FOUNDATIONS for MINISTRY SERIES

Biblical Studies

THE EPISTLE TO THE HEBREWS: PART I

Dr. Don L. Davis

B2-141

TUMI · WORLD IMPACT

The Urban Ministry Institute, a ministry of World Impact, Inc.

The Epistle to the Hebrews: Part I

© 2000, Revised 2015. The Urban Ministry Institute. All Rights Reserved. Copying, redistribution and/or sale of these materials, or any unauthorized transmission, except as may be expressly permitted by the 1976 Copyright Act or in writing from the publisher is prohibited. Requests for permission should be addressed in writing to:

The Urban Ministry Institute
3701 E. 13th Street
Wichita, KS 67208

ISBN: 978-1-62932-414-2

Published by TUMI Press, a division of World Impact, Inc.

The Urban Ministry Institute is a ministry of World Impact, Inc.

The Bible text in this publication, unless otherwise noted, is from the New American Standard Bible. Copyright © 1960, 1962, 1963, 1968, 1971, 1972, 1973, 1975, 1977 by The Lockman Foundation.

Contents

5	About the Author
7	Preface
11	*Session 1* **The Easy Yoke:** Learning of Christ in Biblical Theology
17	*Session 2 • Hebrews 1.1-14* **Christ's Superiority as Revelation and as the Son**
25	*Session 3 • Hebrews 2.1-18* **Christ's Humiliation and Exaltation**
35	*Session 4 • Hebrews 3.1-6* **Christ's Faithfulness as Apostle and High Priest**
43	*Session 5 • Hebrews 3.7-4.13* **Christ's Call to True Discipleship in the New Covenant**
53	*Session 6 • Hebrews 4.14-5.10* **Christ's Perfectly Sympathetic High Priesthood**
61	Appendix
153	Bibliography
157	About Us

About the Author

Rev. Dr. Don L. Davis is the Director of *The Urban Ministry Institute*. He attended Wheaton College and Wheaton Graduate School, and graduated summa cum laude in both his B.A. (1988) and M.A. (1989) degrees, in Biblical Studies and Systematic Theology respectively. He earned his Ph.D. in Religion (Theology and Ethics) from the University of Iowa School of Religion.

In addition to his current duties as the Institute's Director, Dr. Davis also serves as *World Impact's* Senior Vice President of Church and Leadership Development. As such, he oversees the training of urban missionaries, church planters, and city pastors, and facilitates training opportunities for urban Christian workers in evangelism, church growth, and pioneer missions. He also leads the Institute's extensive distance learning programs and facilitates leadership development efforts for organizations and denominations like Prison Fellowship, the Evangelical Free Church of America, and the Church of God in Christ.

A recipient of numerous teaching and academic awards, Dr. Davis has served as professor and faculty at a number of fine academic institutions, having lectured and taught courses in religion, theology, philosophy, and biblical studies at schools such as Wheaton College, St. Ambrose University, the Houston Graduate School of Theology, the University of Iowa School of Religion, the Robert E. Webber Institute of Worship Studies. He has authored a number of books, curricula, and study materials to equip urban leaders, including *The Capstone Curriculum*, TUMI's premiere sixteen-module distance education seminary instruction. Dr. Davis has participated in academic lectureships such as the Staley Lecture series, renewal conferences like the Promise Keepers rallies, and theological consortiums like the University of Virginia Lived Theology Project Series. He received the Distinguished Alumni Fellow Award from the University of Iowa College of Liberal Arts and Sciences in 2009. Dr. Davis is also a member of the Society of Biblical Literature, and the American Academy of Religion.

Preface

The Urban Ministry Institute is a research and leadership development center for World Impact, an interdenominational Christian missions organization dedicated to evangelism and church planting in the inner cities of America. Founded in Wichita, Kansas in 1995, the Institute (TUMI) has sponsored courses, workshops, and leadership training events locally for urban leaders since 1996. We have recorded and reformatted many of these resources over the years, and are now making them available to others who are equipping leaders for the urban church.

Our *Foundations for Ministry Series* represents a significant portion of our on-site training offered to students locally here in Wichita. We are thankful and excited that these materials can now be made available to you. We are confident that you can grow tremendously as you study God's Word and relate its message of justice and grace to your life and ministry.

For your personal benefit, we have included our traditional classroom materials with their corresponding audio recordings of each class session, placing them into a self-study format. We have included extra space in the actual printed materials in order that you may add notes and comments as you listen to the recordings. This will prove helpful as you explore these ideas and topics further.

Remember, the teaching in these sessions was actually given in class and workshop settings at our Hope School of Ministry. This means that, although the workbooks were created for students to follow along and interact with the recordings, some differences may be present. As you engage the material, therefore, please keep in mind that the page numbers on the recordings do not correspond to those in the workbook.

Our earnest prayer is that this *Foundations for Ministry Series* course will prove to be both a blessing and an encouragement to you in your walk with and ministry for Christ. May the Lord so use this course to deepen your knowledge of his Word, in order that you may be outfitted and equipped to complete the task he has for you in kingdom ministry!

This course's main purpose is to help each student better understand the relationship between the two Testaments of Holy Scripture, and how they relate to the person of Jesus of Nazareth as Apostle, Son, High Priest, and God's final revelation.

As a result of taking this course, each student should be able to:
- Quote, interpret, and use effectively key scriptures from Hebrews
- Express how Christ's dynamic salvation gives new meaning to the stories of the Old Testament
- Identify the key issues surrounding Hebrews scholarship
- Explain key doctrines within the book of Hebrews (the nature of salvation, personal holiness, Christian suffering, etc.)
- Communicate the role of typology in Biblical interpretation
- Address central concerns of Christian living and church life through the insights contained in the book of Hebrews

The study of Hebrews is one of the most important studies in Scripture. As a matter of fact, we have selected the book of Hebrews at the Institute as the book that ties both Old and New Testament together in the person and work of Jesus. Hebrews is significant for many reasons. First, it establishes Jesus' divinity as God Son and heir. Second, it shows his fulfillment and superiority over the key Old Testament characters of faith – Moses, Joshua, and Aaron, among others. Perhaps the most important reason is its great detail about the sufficiency and superiority of Christ. This course brings into clear focus the heart message of the Christian faith and its theology. All that God has revealed to us has been in order to show us Christ. Christ is magnificent.

The goal of this course is not just that you understand the different scholarly issues surrounding Hebrews, or some questions we are bound to begin to wrestle with, but a big part of the course is going to be your own love for and walk with Christ. This course should help you grow in your knowledge of Christ, as everything that God wants to do in your life is contingent on your knowledge of this Nazarene. To know Christ is to know life. To literally have Christ, is to have everything God ever wanted to give. Your life, according to the genius of the Bible, will never go beyond your experience of Christ. And so every one of our brief lessons is on Christ, every chapter we are going to study is going to be about him. We study because we are disciples. We want to know him, to love him, to follow him, to live for him and represent him.

> Christ be with me. Christ within me. Christ to win me. Christ to comfort and restore me. Christ beneath me. Christ above me. Christ in quiet. Christ in danger. Christ in hearts of all that love me. Christ in mouth of friend and stranger.
>
> ~ Saint Patrick's Breastplate prayer

And so it is very simple and very profound. Christianity is Christ. Lets seek to understand, to embrace, to love, to be devoted to, to imitate, to cherish, to serve and to obey Christ. The heart of Hebrews is the supremacy and majesty of Christ Jesus as the fulfillment of the revelation of God to the Old Tesament fathers, its Levitical priesthood, its central characters, events, and types, and God's person. This course explores these connections for the sake of spiritual edification and formation.

Don Davis

Assignments and Grading

For our TUMI satellites, all course-relevant materials are located at *www.tumi.org/foundations*.

Each course or workshop has assigned textbooks which are read and discussed throughout the class. We maintain our official *Foundations for Ministry Series* required textbook list at *www.tumi.org/foundationsbooks*.

For more information, please contact us at *foundations@tumi.org*.

Session 1
The Easy Yoke:
Learning of Christ in Biblical Theology

To *accept Christ* is to know the meaning of the words "as He is, so are we in this world." We accept *His* friends as *our* friends, *His* enemies as *our* enemies, *His* ways as *our* ways, *His* rejection as *our* rejection, *His* cross as *our* cross, *His* life as *our* life, and *His* future as *our* future. If this is what we mean when we advise the seeker to accept Christ we had better explain it to him. He may get into deep spiritual trouble unless we do.

~ A. W. Tozer. *That Incredible Christian*.
Harrisburg: Christian Publications, 1964. p. 19.

Give me a fulcrum strong enough and a lever long enough, and I will move the world.

~ Archimedes

I. **Christ, the Center of God's Revelation and Redemption**

  A. As final revelation of *God, the Father*

    1. John 1.14-18

    2. 1 John 1.1-4

    3. John 14.1-8

    4. Col. 2.9-10

    5. Col. 1.15-19

B. As heart of the theology and purpose of the *Holy Scriptures*

1. Luke 24.25-27

2. Luke 24.44-49

3. John 5.39-40

4. Heb. 10.5-7

5. Heb. 1.1-4

C. As the end and *telos* of the *Christian Life* (perfect friendship with Christ)

1. 2 Cor. 3.17-18

2. Matt. 11.28-30

3. Matt. 28.18-20

4. Rom. 8.28-29

5. Eph. 4.9-15

6. 1 John 3.1-3

7. John 15.12-14

John 15.12-14

This is My commandment, that you love one another, just as I have loved you. Greater love has no one than this, that one lay down his life for his friends. You are My friends, if you do what I command you.

Words cannot convey the love which played back and forth like unseen electric impulses between the heart of Jesus and those of His friends. It was a love that sighed, and longed and pitied and hungered. The disciples reached a point where they could not endure being out of His sight. To be near Him was life. To be away from Him was to be out in the lonesome cold. Here was love pure as a mountain stream. It set a new high for love's possibilities among friends. His warmest adorers followed Him when He was popular; they followed Him when the rest had fled. The chief concern of His life seemed to be to make a little circle understand what friendship can really be, to help them see that heaven itself is nothing more than perfect friendship.

~ Frank Laubach. *You Are My Friends*.
New York: Harper and Brothers, 1942. p. 8.

Christ be with me,
Christ within me,
Christ to win me,
Christ to comfort and restore me,
Christ beneath me,
Christ above me,
Christ in quiet,
Christ in danger,
Christ in hearts of all that love me,
Christ in mouth of friend and stranger.

~ St. Patrick, missionary to Ireland, c. 390-c. 461

D. As the substance of God's *kingdom redemption* (in symbol and type)

1. 1 Tim. 2.5-6

2. Isa. 11.1-5; 53.1-12

3. John 1.35-36

4. Heb. 9.11-14

5. 1 Pet. 3.18

6. John 10.10-15

7. Rom. 5.1-11

II. **The Importance of Learning of Christ in Biblical Theology**

A. To enable us to better abide in him

1. We are placed in him.

2. The Christian life is the outworking of our union with him.

....

It is the history of Christ which is to become the experience of the Christian, and we have no spiritual experience apart from Him. The Scriptures tell us that we were "crucified with Him," that we were quickened, raised, and set by God in the heavenlies "in Him," and that we are complete "in Him" (Romans 6.6; Ephesians 2.5-6: Colossians 2.10). It is not just something that is still to be effected in us (though it is that, of course). It is something that has already been effected, in association with Him. In the Scriptures we find that no Christian experience exists as such. What God has done in His gracious purpose is to include us in Christ. In dealing with Christ God has dealt with the Christian; in dealing with the Head He has dealt with all the members. It is altogether wrong for us to think that we can experience anything of the spiritual life in ourselves merely, and apart from Him. God does not intend that we should acquire something exclusively personal in our experience, and He is not willing to effect anything like that for you and me. All the spiritual experience of the Christian is already true in Christ. It has already been experienced by Christ. What we Call "our" experience is only our entering into His history and His experience.

~ Watchman Nee. *The Normal Christian Life*.
Wheaton: Tyndale, 1977. p. 54.

B. To equip us to make disciples of Jesus, Matt. 28.18-20

   1. We give testimony to Christ's sufficiency, 1 Cor. 2.1-5.

   2. We are to teach others all that Christ commanded.

It is inconceivable, therefore, that there could ever be either a higher revelation than God has given through the person of Jesus Christ His Son, or a fuller redemption than He has achieved through the work of Jesus Christ our Savior. Both are perfect and complete. What God has said and did through Jesus Christ He did *hapax*, "once and for all." This is a favorite word in Hebrews with reference to the Cross and is also used by Jude of "the faith which was once for all delivered to the saints." Thus, Christ was offered for our sins once for all, and the faith has been delivered to us once and for all. Please do not misunderstand these affirmations. They do not of course mean that either our understanding or our relationship to God is perfect, but rather that what God has done to make these possible, namely His revelation and redemption through Jesus, are perfect. We have much more to learn, but God has no more to reveal than He has revealed in Jesus Christ. Therefore we shall grow in our Christian understanding as the Holy Spirit enlightens our minds to perceive more of the glory which God has once and for all revealed in Jesus Christ. Again, we have much more to receive, but God has no more to give than He has given in Jesus Christ. Therefore we shall grow our Christian character as the Holy Spirit enables us to claim more of the spiritual inheritance which God has once for all given us in Jesus Christ.

~ John Stott. *Focus on Christ*.
Cleveland: William Collins, 1979. pp. 31-32.

Session 2
Christ's Superiority as Revelation and as the Son:
Hebrews 1.1-14

What then can we say about Hebrews today? Hebrews is a sermon that is rooted in real life. It addresses men and women like ourselves who discover that they can be penetrated by circumstances over which they have no control. It is a sensitive response to the emotional fragileness that characterizes each one of us. It throbs with an awareness of struggle as it explores the dimensions of the cost of discipleship. Hebrews is a pastoral response to the sagging faith of frightened men and women at a time when the imperial capital was striving to regain its composure after the devastation of the great fire. It conveys a word from God addressed to the harsh reality of life in an insecure world. If you have ever felt yourself overwhelmed by that reality, Hebrews is a sermon you cannot afford to neglect.

~ William L. Lane. *Hebrews: A Call to Commitment.*
Peabody: Hendrickson Publishers, 1985. p. 26.

In offering warning and encouragement, which of the following is most important: a sincere heart, good Biblical theology, or a willingness to do the truth?

True or False: It is absolutely essential that if I am to hear God today, I must regularly listen to the preaching of the Word of God in the Church.

What is the best way to bring deliverance, wholeness, and freedom to those for whom we care and to whom we minister?

I. **Introductory Issues with the Book of Hebrews**

   A. Lane's reasons for the theological neglect of Hebrews.

1. Not in the form of an *ancient letter*, p. 15 (*Hebrews: A Call to Commitment*)

2. Its uncertain *setting*, p. 16

3. Its unfamiliar *argument*, p. 16

B. Lane's understanding of the style and substance of Hebrews

1. Hebrews is a *sermon*, p. 17.

2. Hebrews addresses the *cost of discipleship*, p. 20.

3. Hebrews addresses *human frailty*, p. 23.

4. Hebrews is given in *the voice of a friend*, p. 25.

C. General data, p. 1321-27 (*New Bible Commentary*)

1. Who is the *author* of Hebrews?

2. At *what time* was the book written?

3. What *occasion* accompanies the letter, and who are its recipients?

4. What appears to be *its key theme and issue*?

Every carefully structured section contributes to the development of a central theme, providing distinctive insights into the person and work of the Lord Jesus Christ and the nature of our salvation. Although many Old Testament texts are employed, some sections of Hebrews are based on the exposition of a single text, with others being used in a supportive role. In this way we are shown how to interpret the Old Testament in the light of its fulfillment and can understand how the two divisions of the Christian Bible link together. Since the writer regularly relates his insights to the needs of those addressed, we can learn how to apply his argument to our contemporary lives. *Hebrews demonstrates that effective warnings and encouragement are grounded in good theology* (italics mine).

~ *New Bible Commentary.*
Downer's Grove: InterVarsity Press, 1994. p. 1321.

Read Hebrews 1.

II. Jesus Christ, God's Final Word of Revelation to Humankind, Heb. 1.1-4

A. Christ's absolute superiority as revelation: introduction

1. God has spoken decisively through the prophets.

    a. God "spoke of old."

    b. To our "fathers"

    c. By "the prophets"

2. God is speaking to us finally now through his Son, Jesus of Nazareth

   a. In these "last days"

   b. He has spoken "to us"

   c. By "his Son," Jesus Christ

      (1) With OT as preparation for this final revelation, Heb. 8.5; 10.1

      (2) With OT given as analogical shadow to Christ as substance, 1 Cor. 10.1ff.

B. The glorious and incomparable status of the Son as Revelation

   1. The Appointed Heir of all things, Ps. 2.7-8

   2. The Agent through Whom God created the universe, John 1.1-4

   3. The Radiance of God's glorious nature and character, 2 Cor. 4.6

   4. The exact Representation of God's being, Phil. 2.5-11; Col. 2.9-10

   5. Upholder and Sustainer of the created universe through the Word of his power; as Divine Wisdom, Prov. 8.22-31; Col. 1.15-19

6. The Atonement and Sole Deliverer from the defiling character of sin, Heb. 2.14-18

7. The Enthroned Conqueror at the Father's right hand on high, Ps. 110.1

8. Reigning Lord who is superior to the angels

9. Key Implication: Jesus as revelation is supreme to all other forms and manners of God's communication to humankind, John 14.6-8

    a. Creation

    b. Scripture

    c. Conscience

    d. Miracle

    e. Vision

    f. Angels

The Former as Preparatory Revelation	Jesus Christ as God's Final Revelation
At various times and many places	In these last days
God spoke to the fathers	God has spoken to us
In the past	In this final age
Through the prophets	Through his own Son
Adequate but incomplete	Decisively and finally

III. Jesus Christ as Superior to the Angels, Heb. 1.5-14.

A. The *name* of the Son is superior to the name given to the angels.

  1. Jesus is acclaimed uniquely as God's intimate "*My Son*," Ps. 2.7.

  2. Jesus as precise fulfillment of the *Davidic Covenant*, 2 Sam 7.12-16

  3. Jesus' resurrection and ascension give evidence of his unique sonship, Rom. 1.4; Ps. 2.7; Acts 13.33.

B. The *dignity* of the Son is superior to that of the angels.

  1. Angels have never received command to worship other angels, or to receive worship.

  2. The angels are commanded to worship the first born who came into the world as God in the flesh, Deut. 32.42; Ps. 96.7.

  3. As co-equal with God, Jesus receives worship as God, John 5.20-23.

C. The *status and position* of the Son is superior to that of the angels.

  1. The angels are a part of the created order made to carry out God's commands swiftly and powerfully, Ps. 104.4.

  2. The Son of God, however, shares the throne with the Father, as Lord of the kingdom given to him by the Father, Ps. 45.6-7.

3. The Son is over against the creation, and will consummate all things under his divine rule, Ps. 102.25-27.

D. The appointed office of the Son is superior to that of the angels.

1. The Son of God has been invited by the Father to sit at his right hand until all enemies have been defeated, Ps. 110; 1 Cor. 15.23-28.

2. The angels, on the other hand, are ministering spirits to serve the human heirs of salvation, Ps. 103.20; Heb. 5.9.

3. The Son is superior in that he will exercise authority and rule on God's behalf in the Kingdom to come, Luke 1.30-33.

Implications for Life Today

- God is ever speaking to us today in the person of the risen and living Christ, his Son.

- The revelation that God has given to us in Christ is absolutely integrious and veracious (trustworthy and true).

- God has sent his personal angelic emissaries into the world to act on behalf of his children who suffer within it. We are not alone!

- Nothing can defeat or intimidate Christ and his Kingdom victory – nothing!

Session 3
Christ's Humiliation and Exaltation:
Hebrews 2.1-18

I Find My Lord in the Book
I find my Lord in the Bible where ever I chance to look,
He is the theme of the Bible, the center and heart of the Book;
He is the Rose of Sharon, He is the Lily fair,
Where ever I open my Bible, the Lord of the Book is there.

He, at the Book's beginning gave to the earth its form,
He is the Ark of shelter bearing the brunt of the storm,
The Burning Bush of the desert, the budding of Aaron's Rod,
Where ever I look in the Bible, I see the Son of God.

The Ram upon Mt. Moriah, the Ladder from earth to sky,
The Scarlet Cord in the window, and the Serpent lifted high,
The smitten rock in the desert, the Shepherd with staff and crook,
The face of my Lord I discover where ever I open the Book.

He is the Seed of the Woman, the Savior Virgin-born;
He is the Son of David, whom men rejected with scorn,
His garments of grace and of beauty the stately Aaron deck,
Yet He is a priest forever, for He is Melchizedek.

Lord of eternal glory whom John, the Apostle saw;
Light of the golden city, Lamb without spot or flaw,
Bridegroom coming at midnight for whom the Virgins look.
Wherever I open my Bible, I find my Lord in the Book.

~ Author Unknown

When confronted with claims of fact, value, or policy, how does a person prove that they believe a certain claim to be true or false?

True or False: Jesus' humiliation by becoming a human being will be remedied in the Age to Come when he will shed his human form and return to the divine Spirit nature he had with God before he came to earth.

At what point does the revelation that the Lord provides concerning Christ actually begin to influence our thinking, our speaking, our behavior, and our relationships? What turns Biblical truth into dynamic Christian discipleship?

> The fact of our Christian existence is conditioned not by the absence of God but by the presence of God. He makes His presence known through His word and through the gifts He bestows upon the Church. The responsibility of the Christian is to pay the closest attention to the message of salvation delivered through God's Son. That message is the ground of the assurance that God cares deeply for the human family and that He gave himself in love to meet human need.
>
> ~ William L. Lane. *Hebrews: A Call to Commitment.* Peabody: Hendrickson Publishers, 1985. p. 42.

I. **Give Heed to God's Word of Salvation Concerning Christ, Heb. 2.1-4.**

The Implications of the Revelation: the logic arising from the claim of Christ's absolute superiority as Revelation

    A. *The salvific imperative*: pay much closer attention to what we have heard

        1. The word concerning Christ merits attention.

        2. The word concerning Christ merits action.

        3. Lest we *drift away* from it

    B. *The logical proposition*: the unbroken Word of God

        1. The unalterability of the spoken Word

2. The certainty of divine recompense

C. The rhetorical question: How can we escape if we neglect so great a salvation?

1. The greatest certainty and most dreadful tragedy: How precisely *do we neglect* such a great salvation?

    a. Neglect it through *ignorance*

    b. Neglect it through *defiance*

    c. Neglect it through *doubt*

    d. Neglect it through *disregard*

2. "Just look at the kind of word that has been delivered to us!"

    a. It was first spoken through the Lord.

    b. It was confirmed to us by those who heard.

    c. God bore witness through these witnesses.

        (1) Through signs

        (2) Through wonders

        (3) Through various miracles

        (4) Through distributions of the Holy Spirit according to his own will

II. The Divine Intention for Humanity, Heb. 2.5-8

A. The astonishment of the psalmist as to humankind's status, Ps. 8.4-6

1. The world to come was not made subject to angels.

2. The ongoing argument of Christ's superiority veiled in his representative humanity.

   a. The doctrine of "federal headship," Rom. 5

   b. Christ as the Second Adam, 1 Cor. 15

B. The complete picture of our remarkable identity and destiny, Gen. 1.26-28

1. "What is humankind that you are mindful of us?"

2. Made just a little lower than the angels

3. Crowned with glory and honor

4. Appointed as ruler of the works of God's hands

5. Placed all things under his feet

C. All things were subjected to humankind in God's appointment of our dominion; nothing was left out of this subjection.

D. While all things were included, not everything is yet subjected to humankind.

E. Jesus as Son of God in solidarity with humankind as the Representative Human Being, Ps. 8 as prophecy of the dignity of Jesus as Man

   1. Jesus, *the human given name of the Son of God*, Matt. 1.21

   2. Jesus, in becoming a human being, was made *a little lower than the angels*.

   3. Jesus became a human being *for the sake of suffering death*.

   4. Through the grace of God, Jesus participates in our humanity and so *tastes death for everyone*.

III. **Excursus on Using Scriptures Analogically: Criteria for Typological Interpretation**

   A. *Principle #1*: Typological interpretation proper is *Christocentric* in character (i.e. about Christ and his relation to the Scriptural revelation): Jesus is the key to typology.

   1. John 5.39

   2. Heb. 10.7

   3. Matt. 5.17

   4. Luke 24.25-27

   5. Luke 24.44-45

B. *Principle #2*: Typological interpretation is *exploratory* in scope: All dimensions of propositional revelation can be seen as types of Christ.

1. *Historical events*: Noah and the Flood

2. *Biblical figures and characters*: Joseph and his brothers

3. *Ceremonial items*: the Tabernacle and the Temple

4. *Acted liturgies*: Day of Atonement, Lev. 24

5. *Biblical sections*: Moses, Prophets, and the Psalms

6. *Theological symbols*: Ps. 8

7. *Messianic prophecies*: Isa. 53

8. *Metaphors and word pictures*: the Lord is Shepherd, Ps. 23.

9. *Theophanies*: the Angel of the Lord, Gen. 18

10. *Divine manifestations*: Isa. 6; John 12

11. *Allegories*: Gal. 4.21ff.

C. *Principle #3*: Typological interpretation is *narratival* in style: The stories and storylines of the Scriptures are the primary source for typological exegesis.

1. The story of *Noah*: at the level of character and event

2. The story of *Israel*, God's people: at the level of people and nation

3. The story of *Messiah and Kingdom*: at the level of God's unfolding plan of the ages

4. The story of *the triune God and his ultimate intention* for himself: at the level of the person of God alone

IV. **Reasons for the Appropriateness of Jesus' Humiliation and Sharing Our Humanity, Heb. 2.9-18.**

A. For the purpose of *tasting death for everyone*

1. Crowned with glory and honor for the suffering of death

2. Through God's grace, Christ participated in humanity in order to be the substitute for everyone.

B. For the purpose of *bringing many sons and daughters into glory*

1. It was fitting that he for whom all things exist and who made all things.

2. Christ himself as salvation's author was made perfect through human sufferings.

C. For the purpose of sharing with us in *our fundamental humanness under God's rule*

1. The one who sanctifies and those sanctified are one.

2. Christ is not ashamed to call us his very family, his brethren.

    a. Christ declares God's name to his brothers and sisters in the midst of the congregation, Ps. 22.22.

    b. Christ relies on God with us, 2 Sam. 22.3; Isa. 8.17.

    c. "Here I am and the children you gave me," Isa. 8.18.

D. For the purpose of *defeating our adversary, the devil*

   1. *Incredible motive: inasmuch* as the children partook of flesh and blood, so our Savior

   2. *Ironic twist*: Through death Christ destroyed the one who had the power of death, that is, the devil.

   3. *Incisive release*: Release those who through *fear of death* were subject to bondage all their lives

      a. Fear as a snare

      b. Fear of death as the inevitable expectation of all finite beings

      c. Fear as directly related to *bondage*

   4. *Inclusive salvation*: not for angels but for the children of Abraham

E. For the purpose of becoming *a merciful and faithful High Priest* in all things related to God

1. The necessity of Christ's humiliation: "therefore in all things *he had to be made like his brethren.*"

2. As a human being, Christ qualified to be our Mediator to make intercession for us.

    a. He shares our infirmities and identifies with our needs.

    b. He qualifies to be the go-between for God and for us.

    c. Perfectly suited for God and humankind

3. Christ *makes propitiation*: God is appeased through Christ's ministry.

    a. God's demands are satisfied.

    b. Our sins are perfectly atoned for.

4. Christ's human sufferings and temptations equip him to represent humankind perfectly.

    a. He himself has suffered.

    b. He himself was tempted.

    c. *He therefore is able to aid those who are tempted!*

Implications for Life Today

- God's Word has been spoken, confirmed, and authenticated historically and spiritually through the eyewitness testimony and ministry of the apostles.

- We ought to give careful attention to the truth of God's work in Christ or we will drift away from the hope God has offered to us in Christ.

- No one will escape if they disregard this great salvation that God has provided for humankind in Christ; if you refuse Christ, you are on your own in this life, as well as the life to come.

- Christ humbled himself in order to effect God's salvation on our behalf, and express his love and identification with those whom he has redeemed. He is not ashamed to be called our brother!

Session 4
Christ's Faithfulness as Apostle and High Priest:
Hebrews 3.1-6

Apostleship and the Priesthood

What is an *apostle*?

What is a *high priest*?

In representing God and his people, how are their roles *similar*? How are their roles *different*?

What does it mean to *be appointed*, and *to accept an appointment*?

Why would it be absolutely necessary for an apostle and a high priest to be seen as *faithful*?

I. **Command to Consider: Pay Close Attention to Christ Jesus as the Apostle and High Priest of Our Confession, Heb. 3.1.**

The heart of maintaining dynamic faith in a situation of persecution is to become an expert on the person of Jesus Christ as God's Apostle of Revelation and High Priest of Redemption.

   A. *Who we are*: "Holy brethren": the saints of God in Jesus Christ

   1. We are set apart as God's *cherished possession*.

   2. We are set apart for God's *kingdom purpose*.

   3. We are set apart for God's *glorious praise*.

B. *Where we're going*: partakers of the heavenly calling

  1. "I'm goin' up yonder, to be with my Lord!" John 14.1-6.

  2. Called up to the upward prize, Phil. 3.12-14

  3. *Koinonia*, heaven style: partakers of *the heavenly calling*

C. Consider the *Apostle* and *High Priest* of our confession, Christ Jesus.

  1. Why would they need to *consider* him as *Apostle*?

     a. Christ is *an* "apostle" as well as the "apostle": *apostolos*.

     b. His representation is by God's *appointment*.

     c. He is *uniquely representative* of the Father: single definite article "the."

     d. He is the Apostle *of our confession*: one of the core verities which make up our understanding of God's revelation.

  2. Why would they need to *consider* him as *High Priest*?

     a. Christ is a "high priest" as well as *the* "high priest."

     b. His representation is by *God's appointment*.

c. He is *uniquely representative* of the Father: single definite article "the."

d. He is the High Priest of our confession: one of the core verities which make up our understanding of *God's redemption*.

II. **Christ as God's Absolutely Trustworthy Appointee: Christ's Faithfulness to the Father, Heb. 3.2-4**

What is the significance of the fact that Christ was "faithful to him who appointed him"?

A. Christ Jesus was *faithful* to him who *appointed* him.

1. Faithfulness is directly related to the concepts of *authority*, *obedience*, and *commandment*.

2. Christ was *faithful* to the Father, who appointed him, John 10.17.

3. Christ's faithfulness has been and will be *rewarded*, Phil. 2.5-11.

B. Moses' faithful stewardship over God's house is a *type* of Christ.

1. Moses was faithful in all of God's house.

a. Faithful in his *representation*: Moses was faithful in the integrity of his ambassadorship for God to the people.

b. Faithful in his *intercession*: Moses was faithful in his persistent pleas for God on behalf of the people.

c. Faithful in his *availability*: Moses was faithful in his unconditional availability to the Father.

d. Faithful in his *longevity*: Moses was faithful until death.

2. Christ's faithful representation is *greater than Moses'*.

   a. Christ's ministry is more glorious than the ministry of Moses.

   b. Christ Jesus built the house.

   c. As builder of the house, he is worthy of greater honor than the house itself (and any stewarding ministry associated with it).

3. The Builder of all things: The relationship of the members within the Trinity, ". . . but he who built all things is God."

   a. The Father *establishes* the purposes of God's revelation and redemption through his perfect plan.

   b. The Son *executed* the purposes of God's revelation and redemption, which the Father planned.

   c. The Holy Spirit *expresses* the purposes of God's revelation and redemption, which the Father planned and the Son executed.

III. Contrasting the Faithful Ministries of Moses and Christ Jesus, Heb. 3.5-6

As stated earlier, to study Bible types is essentially to relate the person of Christ to the different phenomena in the Bible *before his appearance*. The key to typological interpretation of Scripture is the need to determine exactly in what way and in what manner does the person of Christ resonate with the character, event, symbol, or happening in the Old Testament. Typological interpretation, therefore, is largely *a procedure of understanding how to contrast and compare Christ and the facts of the Hebrew Scriptures.*

A. *Moses'* faithful stewardship over God's House

1. Faithful in all of *God's house*

2. Functioned as a *servant* in God's house

3. Moses' ministry served as a *testimony* of those things which would be spoken of afterward.

B. *Christ Jesus'* faithful stewardship over his own house

1. Faithful over *his own house*; the "house" over which Jesus is absolutely faithful, in perfect obedience to the command of the Father, are the saints of the living God in Christ. We ourselves are the very house of God.

2. Functions as God's only begotten *Son*

3. Whose *house we are!* (Believers in Christ are literally "Up in the House").

    a. We are the *temple* of God, 1 Cor. 3.16-17; 6.19-20; Eph. 2.19-22.

      b. We are the *household* of God, Gal. 6.10.

      c. We are the *family* of God, Eph. 5.1-2; Acts 17.24ff.

C. *Imitating Jesus*: the condition of being the "house" of God

  1. We are God's house with specific conditions attached.

  2. We must hold fast *the confidence* to the end.

      a. We must know what we believe.

      b. We must hold fast the confidence of its truthfulness.

      c. We must hold this conviction to the end (not backslide or turn back).

  3. We must hold fast *the rejoicing of the hope* firm to the end.

      a. We must look forward to the consummation.

      b. We must hold fast the promise of its coming.

      c. We must hold this vision of the future firm to the end (and not substitute it with a less noble, worldly vision here).

  4. The implicit Christo-centric impulse: As Christ was faithful to the end, so we who belong to him, must strive to be faithful to the end.

Moses as Faithful Servant	Christ Jesus as Faithful Son
Faithful over God's house	Faithful over his own house
Functioned as servant	Functions as God's Son
Faithful in God's affairs	Faithful over his own people
A Testimony of Things to Come	The Reality the Testimony prefigured
Worthy of honor	Worthy of great glory and honor

Implications for Life Today

- Christ Jesus is the Absolutely Trustworthy Representative of the Father's Revelation and Redemption.

- As Apostle, Jesus is God's single messenger giving us God's mind, and as High Priest Jesus is God's single intercessor serving before the Father as our daysman (go-between).

- Typological interpretation, therefore, is largely a procedure of understanding how to contrast and compare Christ and the facts of the Hebrew Scriptures.

- Christ Jesus serves his Father as a Faithful Representative to give stewardship and care over God's house, whose house we are if we continue to hold fast our confidence and hope to the end.

Session 5
Christ's Call to True Discipleship in the New Covenant:
Hebrews 3.7-4.13

Hardness of heart signifies treating the Lord with contempt; it is the refusal to believe in the Lord; it is choosing to listen to human voices of despair rather than listening to the voice of God.

~ William L. Lane. *Hebrews: A Call to Commitment.* Peabody: Hendrickson Publishers, 1985. p. 64.

Jesus – Do You Believe in Him?
A man who was merely a man and said the sort of things Jesus said would not be a great moral teacher. He would either be a lunatic-on a level with the man who says he is a poached egg-or else he would be the Devil of Hell.

You must make your choice.

Either this man was, and is, the Son of God: or else a madman or something worse. You can shut Him up for a fool, you can spit at Him and kill Him as a demon; or you can fall at His feet and call Him Lord and God. But let us not come with any patronizing nonsense about His being a great human teacher. He has not left that open to us. He did not intend to.

~ C. S. Lewis. *Mere Christianity.* New York: Macmillan, 1952. p. 56.

Hast Thou No Scar?
Hast thou no scar?
No hidden scar on foot, or side, or hand?
I hear thee sung as mighty in the land.
I hear them hail thy bright ascendant star.
Has thou no scar?

Hast thou no wound?
Yet I was wounded by the archers, spent,
Leaned Me against a tree to die; and rent
By ravening beasts that compassed Me,
I swooned;
Has thou no wound?

No wound, no scar?
Yet, as the Master shall the servant be,
And pierced are the feet that follow Me;
But thine are whole; can he have followed far
Who has no wound or scar?

~ Amy Carmichael

I. **Living the Intersection: Bringing to Bear Israel's Experience in Our Lives Today**

A. The experience of Israel as tutor to our discipleship

1. Israel's experience is given as *example not to follow*.

2. God offers Israel's experience as *tutorial model*.

3. The Hebrew Scriptures are written for our *admonition*.

B. Lane's understanding of the author's choice of Psalm 95.7-11

1. This passage was *familiar*, p. 61 (*Hebrews: A Call to Commitment*).

2. This passage was a *sober reminder of the unfaithfulness of the people of God*, p. 62.

3. This passage stresses the priority of *listening to God's voice*, p. 62.

4. This passage underscores both the *peril of unbelief and the tragic consequences of unfaithfulness*, p. 62.

C. The *power of story* in discipling and teaching.

1. *Shows the truth* rather than merely tells it; provides a living visual aid

2. Gives a *window into the world of God's disposition* and understanding

3. *Of greater interest and is more entertaining* than mere outline and prose material

4. A thicker kind of experience: allows us *to participate*: empathy, emotion, feeling, passion

5. *Easier to remember and to teach* to others than mere propositions

II. Christ's Call to Faithfulness: Enter into the Promised Land by Faith, Heb. 3.7-19.

> The problem of a living faith, of faith without doubt, is a very real one. Many who have deep devotional habits and who live disciplined lives of prayer and intercession are never quite sure that they have prevailed because their faith seems tentative, dim, uncertain, and often mixed with doubt. Large segments of the Body of Christ are baffled by this plague. Much of the effectiveness of many well-organized prayer programs is crippled by failure to reach a triumphant faith. Since few know how to obtain and exercise this achieving faith, many prayer efforts bog down in frustration and defeat.
>
> ~ Paul Billheimer. *Destined for the Throne.* Minneapolis: Bethany House, 1996. p. 115.

A. Recitation of Psalms 95.7-11; Hebrews 3.7-11.

  1. This passage as the *"official midrash"* (commentary) on Psalm 95.7-11.

      a. Regularly used in the *synagogue liturgy*

      b. Already *known to most first-century Jews* who recited the Psalms

  2. Insight into the *role of Scripture* in the discipling process

B. *Midrash upon midrash*: Psalm 95 as midrash on the account of Israel at Kadesh-Barnea, Num. 13-14

  1. The prospect of *entering and possessing the land*, Num. 13.1-2

2. *The calling of the spies* and the strategic scouting mission, Num. 13.17-20

3. *Forty days of scouting*: the land flowing with milk and honey, Num. 13.24-27

4. The *evil report* of the ten spies, Num. 13.28-32

5. *Joshua and Caleb*: men of Kingdom vision, Num. 13.30; 14.6-9

6. Unbelief, despair, rebellion, and *hardness of heart*, Num. 14.1-10

7. God's threats, Moses' intercession, and *God's forgiveness*, Num. 14.13-20

8. *God's terrifying judgment* on unbelief, Num. 14.21-35

9. *Too little response too late*: defeat and lost time, Num. 14.39-45

C. The Analogical Imagination: As it was *with Israel*, so it may be *with us* if we do not believe the Lord.

1. *Be on your guard* lest any of you get a hardened heart of unbelief.

   a. *You* can become a victim to the despair and rebellion associated with unbelief.

   b. Unbelief is seen in God's mind as *departing from him*.

2. Exhort each other *every day*, while it is called "Today."

   a. The significance of *daily* exhortation

   b. All of us are subject to the *hardness which comes through unbelief*.

   c. All sin has a *deceitful root*: sin and deception are connected.

3. Partakers of Christ: the need to hold on to *our confidence to the end*

4. Make the connection in the logic of the story.

   a. *Who* were those who rebelled? *The same ones* led by God's man who witnessed God's deliverance!

   b. *With whom* was God angry? *The same ones* who doubted his promise and who died in the wilderness!

   c. *To whom* did he swear they would never enter into the rest of the Promised land? *The same ones* who heard his promise because of unbelief and disobedience.

5. The power of *unbelief*

Israel and Their Unbelief	The Hebrews and Their Need to Believe
Heard the Word of the Lord	Heard the Word of Christ
Were on the threshold of Canaan	Were on the threshold of Christ
Were hardened due to unbelief	Can be hardened by unbelief
Disobeyed God's commands	Were vacillating with God's commands
Deceived and despaired	Warned and exhorted

III. Entering into the Rest of God's New Covenant of Promise, Heb. 4.1-13

A. The *promise* of God's rest

1. *Privilege and responsibility*: believing the Gospel preached

    a. The proper attitude in the face of unbelief: *fear*

    b. The Gospel preached to us all: *the catalytic power of faith*

    c. The key to *spiritual profit*: mixing the Word heard with faith

2. *Faith as the condition* of entering into the promise of God's rest

3. Biblical allusions to the *promise*

   a. God's *Sabbath rest*, Gen. 2.2

   b. God's *spiritual rest*, Ps. 95.11

B. The *Day* of God's rest: "*Today*, if you will hear his voice"

1. The failure of the disobedient to enter God's rest

2. God's designation of a certain *day*, Ps. 95.7-8

3. God's Sabbath rest for the people of God

   a. The call to discipleship is a call to *freedom and rest*, Gal. 5.1.

   b. The *paradox* of the New covenant: created unto good works while ceasing *from* one's own work.

   c. We cease *as* God did from his.

C. Forceful conclusion: *Be diligent to Enter God's rest.*

1. Be diligent because *any of us can fall* after the same example of disobedience.

2. Be diligent because *the Word of God is potent.*

   a. It is *living* and *powerful.*

   b. Sharper than any *two-edged sword*

   c. *Discerner* of the thoughts and intents of the heart

3. Be diligent because *nothing and no one is hidden* from his sight.

Implications for Life Today

- If you hear God's voice, believe his Word about Christ. Do not harden your heart.

- As God dealt with his people Israel, so God will deal with us.

- The call to discipleship is a call to God's covenant rest. God has finished his work in Christ, which we embrace by faith.

- Exhort one another every day, while it is called "Today," to be diligent to enter into God's rest -- unbelievers will not enter into God's rest.

Session 6
Christ's Perfectly Sympathetic High Priesthood
Hebrews 4.14-5.10

He Dies! The Friend of Sinners Dies!
He dies! The Friend of sinners dies!
Lo! Salem's daughters weep around;
A solemn darkness veils the skies,
A sudden trembling shakes the ground:
Come, saints, and drop a tear or two
For Him who groan'd beneath your load;
He shed a thousand drops for you,
A thousand drops of richer blood.

Here's love and grief beyond degree:
The Lord of glory dies for man!
But lo! What sudden joys we see:
Jesus, the dead, revives again.
The rising God forsakes the tomb;
(In vain the tomb forbids His rise;)
Cherubic legions guard Him home,
And shout Him welcome to the skies.

Break off your tears, ye saints, and tell
How high your great Deliv'rer reigns;
Sing how He spoil'd the hosts of hell,
And led the monster death in chains:
Say, "Live forever, wondrous King!
Born to redeem, and strong to save;"
Then ask the monster, "Where's thy sting?"
And, "Where's thy victry, boasting grave?"

~ Isaac Watts, 1674-1748

> "For we do *not* have a high priest who is *not* able to feel our weaknesses with us." Stated positively, He is able to feel what we feel. He is able to feel our weaknesses with us because He shared the situation in which we find ourselves. That explains why His high priestly ministry of intercession on our behalf is effective. . . . *our high priest suffers together with the one who is being tested, and brings active help.* When the lash is falling on you, He rushes in so that it falls upon Him as well. When you are treated with contempt, He experiences the humiliation that you feel. When you are bruised, He feels the pain. *He is able to feel our weaknesses with us.*
>
> ~ William L. Lane. *Hebrews: A Call to Commitment.* Peabody: Hendrickson Publishers, 1985. p. 75.

What is the character of Christ's high priestly ministry before God on our behalf?

How does Christ's ability to empathize with us guarantee the effectiveness of his ministry for us?

Why is suffering a component in the growth and development of any maturing disciple of Christ, and how do we help ourselves and others prepare for this inevitability?

I. **Christ's Perfect Identification with the Weariness, Suffering, and Defenselessness of the Church**

   A. The reason for our holding fast our confession in the midst of struggle and pain: Our high priest, *Jesus the Son of God*, has passed through the heavens.

   B. Lane's analysis: Hebrews 4.14-16 as commentary on 2.17-18 (pp. 74-75, *Hebrews: A Call to Commitment*)

      1. Christ's *oneness with God's people*

      2. Christ's priestly *compassion* as exercised in God's service

3. Christ's personal *testing* as experienced in death

4. Christ's ability to *secure those going through ordeals* because of his empathy with them

5. Lane's understanding of Hebrews 4.15-16 is to "announce the perspectives developed in 5.1-10 (p. 75).

C. Christ as the perfect *identifier with* and *helper of* the helpless

1. Christ's ability to feel, to sympathize, *to suffer along* with our weaknesses (i.e. compassion)

2. Christ's compassion is connected to *Christ's full humanity*.

    a. He was *fully human*, "tempted in all things as we are," John 1.14-18.

        (1) Were Jesus' temptations like ours?

        (2) Could Jesus have given in to temptation – could Jesus have sinned if he had chosen to do so?

    b. He was exposed to *"the full range of human testing,"* Lev. 24 (p. 76, *Hebrews: A Call to Commitment*).

    c. Christ *resonates* with our weakness since his suffering was in concert with and very much like our own.

D. The *prayer of boldness* that accompanies the realization of Christ's perfect identification.

1. The characteristic of one who understands Christ's identification: *draw near to the throne of grace with boldness!*

2. Allusion to the *Day of Atonement* (Christ makes it possible for all believers to enter God's presence boldly now), p. 76 (*Hebrews: A Call to Commitment*).

3. *Worship and grateful supplication*: the knowledge of gaining immediate, unbroken access to God

4. Receiving a thicker kind of experience: allows us *to participate*: empathy, emotion, feeling, passion

II. Christ's Intercession and Advocacy: The Sympathetic and Faithful High Priest, Heb. 5.1-10.

The office of the high priest is characterized by his title. He was the spiritual head of his people, but since the period of the Hasmoneans he added the regal crown to the ecclesiastical mitre. His participation in the sacrificial duties during the year was left to his discretion, but he was supposed to act as offering priest on the Day of Atonement. There is no reason to assume that even on the day he nominated any other priest for his work, as otherwise the Mishnah would have had no cause to describe the preparations which began a week beforehand, when he had to make himself familiar with the details of his task for the holy day. . . . the service itself, which claimed his undivided attention and included the fast, five baths, and ten lavings of hands and feet, must have made great demands on his physical strength. When we add to this the anxiety not to commit a mistake, we can understand the Mishnaic allusion to the satisfaction expressed at the close of the Day (Yoma, vii 4).

~ James Hastings, ed. *Encyclopedia of Religion and Ethics*, Vol. 10. New York: Charles Scribner's Sons, 1961. p. 322-23.

A. Six central traits of the Aaronic high priesthood.

Note: Lane's identification of the concentric symmetry of the author's argument here is important (p. 77).

The *old office* of high priest (Heb. 5.1)
The *solidarity* of priest with the people (5.2-3)
The *humility* of the high priest (5.4)
The *humility* of Christ (5.5-6)
The *solidarity* of Christ with the people (5.7-8)
The *new office* of high priest (5.9-10)

1. The high priest is "taken from among the people."

2. The high priest is "appointed on behalf of the people in things pertaining to God."

3. The high priest is commissioned "to offer both gifts and sacrifices for sins."

4. The high priest is called to "deal gently with the ignorant and misguided."

    a. This capacity is ingredient in the call of the priest.

    b. This responsibility is able to be accomplished because "he himself also is beset with weakness."

5. The high priest is obligated to offer sacrifices for sins, as for the people and so also for himself *because of their mutual neediness.*

6. The high priest does not take this honor upon himself, but receives it as a result of the calling of God.

    a. God's initiative is critical.

    b. The Aaronic priesthood is a clear illustration, 2 Chron. 26.18; Exod. 28.1ff)

B. Christ's fulfillment of, superiority over, and extension beyond the Aaronic high priesthood

1. Christ did not glorify himself by self appointment to this office of high priest but was *appointed by the Father*.

2. What is the relationship between Christ's *sonship* and his *high priestly* office? "Thou art my Son, today I have begotten Thee," Ps. 2.7.

3. How does Psalm 110.4 demonstrate for the author *the superiority of Christ's priesthood*? "Thou art a priest forever according to the order of Melchizedek," Ps. 110.4.

C. The *confession* of the priestly nature of Christ's life

1. In the days of his flesh, Jesus' prayers and supplications were *offerings to God*, p. 81 (*Hebrews: A Call to Commitment*).

    a. The *manner* of his offerings: made with loud crying and tears

    b. The *object* of his offerings: to the One able to save him from death

    c. The *result* of his offerings: He was heard because of his piety.

2. Although Christ was a Son (therefore heir and Lord), he *learned obedience* through the things he *suffered*.

    a. His exalted status was *given*, his obedience *learned*.

b. The things he *suffered* were the tutor of his learned obedience, p. 82.

3. Christ now has become the source of eternal salvation.

a. Christ *was made perfect* in all of the testings he endured.

b. Through his perfection Christ can now become *the source of eternal salvation* for those who *obey* him.

4. Christ's new office (superior to Aaronic office) is the priesthood according to *the order of Melchizedek*.

Insights for Today

- We ought to hold fast our confession because our high priest, Jesus the Son of God, sympathizes with our weaknesses, at our deepest and most fundamental levels.

- Jesus was tempted in all ways as we are, yet he never gave in to those temptations even a single instance, whether in thought, word, or deed.

- We can come to the throne of grace boldly, with grateful worship and confident anticipation of blessing because Jesus has become the source of eternal salvation (past, present, and future).

- We should know that no struggle, fight, weakness, infirmity, problem, or need we face was not felt by Christ himself during his time here on the earth. He is fully human.

- Jesus fulfilled, extended, and is superior to the high priestly order of Aaron, and has been appointed to the order of Melchizedek (no beginning or end, always potent, and final).

Appendix

65 **Appendix 1**
The Nicene Creed

66 **Appendix 2**
The Nicene Creed With Biblical Support

68 **Appendix 3**
We Believe: Confession of the Nicene Creed (8.7.8.7. Meter*)

69 **Appendix 4**
We Believe: Confession of the Nicene Creed (Common Meter*)

70 **Appendix 5**
The Story of God: Our Sacred Roots

71 **Appendix 6**
Once upon a Time

74 **Appendix 7**
The Theology of Christus Victor

75 **Appendix 8**
Christus Victor: An Integrated Vision for the Christian Life

76 **Appendix 9**
Old Testament Witness to Christ and His Kingdom

77 **Appendix 10**
Summary Outline of the Scriptures

81 **Appendix 11**
From Before to Beyond Time

84 **Appendix 12**
There Is a River

85 **Appendix 13**
A Schematic for a Theology of the Kingdom of God

86 **Appendix 14**
Living in the Already and the Not Yet Kingdom

87 **Appendix 15**
Jesus of Nazareth: The Presence of the Future

88	**Appendix 16** Traditions (*Paradosis*)
96	**Appendix 17** Documenting Your Work
100	**Appendix 18** Representin': Jesus as God's Chosen Representative
101	**Appendix 19** Faithfully Re-presenting Jesus of Nazareth
102	**Appendix 20** Messianic Prophecies Cited in the New Testament
108	**Appendix 21** Ethics of the New Testament: Living in the Upside-Down Kingdom of God
109	**Appendix 22** Preaching and Teaching Jesus of Nazareth as Messiah and Lord Is the Heart of All Biblical Ministry
110	**Appendix 23** Summary of Messianic Interpretations in the Old Testament
115	**Appendix 24** Suffering for the Gospel: The Cost of Discipleship and Servant-Leadership
117	**Appendix 25** Messiah Yeshua in Every Book of the Bible
119	**Appendix 26** Old Testament Names, Titles, and Epithets for the Messiah
121	**Appendix 27** Messiah Jesus: Fulfillment of the Old Testament Types
125	**Appendix 28** The Shadow and the Substance: Understanding the Old Testament as God's Witness to Jesus Christ
126	**Appendix 29** Analytical vs. Christocentric Approach to Old Testament Study

127	**Appendix 30** From Deep Ignorance to Credible Witness: Stages of Dynamic Growth
128	**Appendix 31** In Christ
129	**Appendix 32** Substitute Centers to a Christ-Centered Vision
130	**Appendix 33** The Picture and the Drama: Image and Story in the Recovery of Biblical Myth
131	**Appendix 34** Union with Christ: The Christocentric Paradigm
134	**Appendix 35** Typology
137	**Appendix 36** Typology Readings
143	**Appendix 37** With Him
144	**Appendix 38** Focus on Christ
145	**Appendix 39** Theological Support for the Position That Jesus Could Have Sinned Had He Chosen to Do So
147	**Appendix 40** The Tabernacle of Moses
148	**Appendix 41** Arrangement of the Twelve Tribes around the Tabernacle
149	**Appendix 42** The Two Movements of Christ's Revelation: The Humiliation and Exaltation of the Son of God
150	**Appendix 43** The Mystery of God: The Word Made Flesh in Jesus Christ

151 **Appendix 44**
The Risen Messiah Himself Is Our Life

152 **Appendix 45**
Major Heresies Concerning the Lord Jesus Christ

Appendix 1
The Nicene Creed
The Urban Ministry Institute

We believe in one God, the Father Almighty, Maker of heaven and earth and of all things visible and invisible.

We believe in one Lord Jesus Christ, the only Begotten Son of God, begotten of the Father before all ages, God from God, Light from Light, True God from True God, begotten not created, of the same essence as the Father, through whom all things were made.

Who for us men and for our salvation came down from heaven and was incarnate by the Holy Spirit and the Virgin Mary and became human. Who for us too, was crucified under Pontius Pilate, suffered and was buried. The third day he rose again according to the Scriptures, ascended into heaven, and is seated at the right hand of the Father. He will come again in glory to judge the living and the dead, and his Kingdom will have no end.

We believe in the Holy Spirit, the Lord and life-giver, who proceeds from the Father and the Son, who together with the Father and Son is worshiped and glorified, who spoke by the prophets.

We believe in one holy, catholic, and apostolic Church.

We acknowledge one baptism for the forgiveness of sin, and we look for the resurrection of the dead and the life of the age to come. Amen.

Appendix 2
The Nicene Creed With Biblical Support
The Urban Ministry Institute

We believe in one God, *(Deut. 6.4-5; Mark 12.29; 1 Cor. 8.6)*
    the Father Almighty, *(Gen. 17.1; Dan. 4.35; Matt. 6.9; Eph. 4.6; Rev. 1.8)*
    Maker of heaven and earth *(Gen. 1.1; Isa. 40.28; Rev. 10.6)*
    and of all things visible and invisible. *(Ps. 148; Rom. 11.36; Rev. 4.11)*

We believe in one Lord Jesus Christ, the only Begotten Son of God, begotten of the Father before all ages, God from God, Light from Light, True God from True God, begotten not created, of the same essence as the Father,
    (John 1.1-2; 3.18; 8.58; 14.9-10; 20.28; Col. 1.15, 17; Heb. 1.3-6)
    through whom all things were made. *(John 1.3; Col. 1.16)*

Who for us men and for our salvation came down from heaven and was incarnate by the Holy Spirit and the Virgin Mary and became human.
    (Matt. 1.20-23; John 1.14; 6.38; Luke 19.10)
    Who for us too, was crucified under Pontius Pilate, suffered and was buried.
    (Matt. 27.1-2; Mark 15.24-39, 43-47; Acts 13.29; Rom. 5.8; Heb. 2.10; 13.12)
    The third day he rose again according to the Scriptures,
    (Mark 16.5-7; Luke 24.6-8; Acts 1.3; Rom. 6.9; 10.9; 2 Tim. 2.8)
    ascended into heaven, and is seated at the right hand of the Father.
    (Mark 16.19; Eph. 1.19-20)
    He will come again in glory to judge the living and the dead, and his Kingdom will have no end. *(Isa. 9.7; Matt. 24.30; John 5.22; Acts 1.11; 17.31; Rom. 14.9; 2 Cor. 5.10; 2 Tim. 4.1)*

We believe in the Holy Spirit, the Lord and life-giver, *(Gen. 1.1-2; Job 33.4; Ps. 104.30; 139.7-8; Luke 4.18-19; John 3.5-6; Acts 1.1-2; 1 Cor. 2.11; Rev. 3.22)*
    who proceeds from the Father and the Son, *(John 14.16-18, 26; 15.26; 20.22)*
    who together with the Father and Son is worshiped and glorified,
    (Isa. 6.3; Matt. 28.19; 2 Cor. 13.14; Rev. 4.8)
    who spoke by the prophets. *(Num. 11.29; Mic. 3.8; Acts 2.17-18; 2 Pet. 1.21)*

We believe in one holy, catholic, and apostolic Church.
    (Matt. 16.18; Eph. 5.25-28; 1 Cor. 1.2; 10.17; 1 Tim. 3.15; Rev. 7.9)

We acknowledge one baptism for the forgiveness of sin, *(Acts 22.16; 1 Pet. 3.21; Eph. 4.4-5)*
    And we look for the resurrection of the dead and the life of the age to come.
    (Isa. 11.6-10; Mic. 4.1-7; Luke 18.29-30; Rev. 21.1-5; 21.22-22.5)
    Amen.

The Nicene Creed with Biblical Support, continued

Memory Verses

Below are suggested memory verses, one for each section of the Creed.

The Father — Rev. 4.11 (ESV) – Worthy are you, our Lord and God, to receive glory and honor and power, for you created all things, and by your will they existed and were created.

The Son — John 1.1 (ESV) – In the beginning was the Word, and the Word was with God, and the Word was God.

The Son's Mission — 1 Cor. 15.3-5 (ESV) – For what I received I passed on to you as of first importance: that Christ died for our sins according to the Scriptures, that he was buried, that he was raised on the third day according to the Scriptures, and that he appeared to Peter, and then to the Twelve.

The Holy Spirit — Rom. 8.11 (ESV) – If the Spirit of him who raised Jesus from the dead dwells in you, he who raised Christ Jesus from the dead will also give life to your mortal bodies through his Spirit who dwells in you.

The Church — 1 Pet. 2.9 (ESV) – But you are a chosen race, a royal priesthood, a holy nation, a people for his own possession, that you may proclaim the excellencies of him who called you out of darkness into his marvelous light.

Our Hope — 1 Thess. 4.16-17 (ESV) – For the Lord himself will descend from heaven with a cry of command, with the voice of an archangel, and with the sound of the trumpet of God. And the dead in Christ will rise first. Then we who are alive, who are left, will be caught up together with them in the clouds to meet the Lord in the air, and so we will always be with the Lord.

Appendix 3
We Believe: Confession of the Nicene Creed
(8.7.8.7. Meter*)
Rev. Dr. Don L. Davis, 2007

* This song is adapted from the Nicene Creed, and set to 8.7.8.7. meter, meaning it can be sung to tunes of the same meter, such as: Joyful, Joyful, We Adore Thee; I Will Sing of My Redeemer; What a Friend We Have in Jesus; Come, Thou Long Expected Jesus

Father God Almighty rules, the Maker of both earth and heav'n.
All things seen and those unseen, by him were made, by him were giv'n!
We believe in Jesus Christ, the Lord, God's one and only Son,
Begotten, not created, too, he and our Father God are one!

Begotten from the Father, same, in essence, as both God and Light;
Through him by God all things were made, in him all things were giv'n life.
Who for us all, for our salvation, did come down from heav'n to earth,
Incarnate by the Spirit's pow'r, and through the Virgin Mary's birth.

Who for us too, was crucified, by Pontius Pilate's rule and hand,
Suffered, and was buried, yet on the third day, he rose again.
According to the Sacred Scriptures all that happ'ned was meant to be.
Ascended high to God's right hand, in heav'n he sits in glory.

Christ will come again in glory to judge all those alive and dead.
His Kingdom rule shall never end, for he will rule and reign as Head.
We worship God, the Holy Spirit, Lord and the Life-giver known;
With Fath'r and Son is glorified, Who by the prophets ever spoke.

And we believe in one true Church, God's holy people for all time,
Cath'lic in its scope and broadness, built on the Apostles' line!
Acknowledging that one baptism, for forgiv'ness of our sin,
And we look for Resurrection, for the dead shall live again.

Looking for unending days, the life of the bright Age to come,
When Christ's Reign shall come to earth, the will of God shall then be done!
Praise to God, and to Christ Jesus, to the Spirit–triune Lord!
We confess the ancient teachings, clinging to God's holy Word!

Appendix 4
We Believe: Confession of the Nicene Creed
(Common Meter)*
Rev. Dr. Don L. Davis, 2007

* This song is adapted from the Nicene Creed, and set to common meter (8.6.8.6.), meaning it can be sung to tunes of the same meter, such as: O, for a Thousand Tongues to Sing; Alas, and Did My Savior Bleed; Amazing Grace; All Hail the Power of Jesus' Name; There Is a Fountain; Joy to the World

The Father God Almighty rules, Maker of earth and heav'n.
Yes, all things seen and those unseen, by him were made, and given!

We hold to one Lord Jesus Christ, God's one and only Son,
Begotten, not created, too, he and our Lord are one!

Begotten from the Father, same, in essence, God and Light;
Through him all things were made by God, in him were given life.

Who for us all, for salvation, came down from heav'n to earth,
Was incarnate by the Spirit's pow'r, and the Virgin Mary's birth.

Who for us too, was crucified, by Pontius Pilate's hand,
Suffered, was buried in the tomb, on third day rose again.

According to the Sacred text all this was meant to be.
Ascended to heav'n, to God's right hand, now seated high in glory.

He'll come again in glory to judge all those alive and dead.
His Kingdom rule shall never end, for he will reign as Head.

We worship God, the Holy Spirit, our Lord, Life-giver known,
With Fath'r and Son is glorified, Who by the prophets spoke.

And we believe in one true Church, God's people for all time,
Cath'lic in scope, and built upon the apostolic line.

Acknowledging one baptism, for forgiv'ness of our sin,
We look for Resurrection day–the dead shall live again.

We look for those unending days, life of the Age to come,
When Christ's great Reign shall come to earth, and God's will shall be done!

Appendix 5
The Story of God: Our Sacred Roots
Rev. Dr. Don L. Davis

The Alpha and the Omega	Christus Victor	Come, Holy Spirit	Your Word Is Truth	The Great Confession	His Life in Us	Living in the Way	Reborn to Serve
The LORD God is the source, sustainer, and end of all things in the heavens and earth. All things were formed and exist by his will and for his eternal glory, the triune God, Father, Son, and Holy Spirit, Rom. 11.36.							
The Triune God's Unfolding Drama — God's Self-Revelation in Creation, Israel, and Christ				The Church's Participation in God's Unfolding Drama — Fidelity to the Apostolic Witness to Christ and His Kingdom			
The Objective Foundation: The Sovereign Love of God — God's Narration of His Saving Work in Christ				The Subjective Practice: Salvation by Grace through Faith — The Redeemed's Joyous Response to God's Saving Work in Christ			
The Author of the Story	The Champion of the Story	The Interpreter of the Story	The Testimony of the Story	The People of the Story	Re-enactment of the Story	Embodiment of the Story	Continuation of the Story
The Father as Director	Jesus as Lead Actor	The Spirit as Narrator	Scripture as Script	As Saints, Confessors	As Worshipers, Ministers	As Followers, Sojourners	As Servants, Ambassadors
Christian Worldview	Communal Identity	Spiritual Experience	Biblical Authority	Orthodox Theology	Priestly Worship	Congregational Discipleship	Kingdom Witness
Theistic and Trinitarian Vision	Christ-centered Foundation	Spirit-Indwelt and -Filled Community	Canonical and Apostolic Witness	Ancient Creedal Affirmation of Faith	Weekly Gathering in Christian Assembly	Corporate, Ongoing Spiritual Formation	Active Agents of the Reign of God
Sovereign Willing	Messianic Representing	Divine Comforting	Inspired Testifying	Truthful Retelling	Joyful Excelling	Faithful Indwelling	Hopeful Compelling
Creator True Maker of the Cosmos	Recapitulation Typos and Fulfillment of the Covenant	Life-Giver Regeneration and Adoption	Divine Inspiration God-breathed Word	The Confession of Faith Union with Christ	Song and Celebration Historical Recitation	Pastoral Oversight Shepherding the Flock	Explicit Unity Love for the Saints
Owner Sovereign Disposer of Creation	Revealer Incarnation of the Word	Teacher Illuminator of the Truth	Sacred History Historical Record	Baptism into Christ Communion of Saints	Homilies and Teachings Prophetic Proclamation	Shared Spirituality Common Journey through the Spiritual Disciplines	Radical Hospitality Evidence of God's Kingdom Reign
Ruler Blessed Controller of All Things	Redeemer Reconciler of All Things	Helper Endowment and the Power	Biblical Theology Divine Commentary	The Rule of Faith Apostles' Creed and Nicene Creed	The Lord's Supper Dramatic Re-enactment	Embodiment Anamnesis and Prolepsis through the Church Year	Extravagant Generosity Good Works
Covenant Keeper Faithful Promisor	Restorer Christ, the Victor over the powers of evil	Guide Divine Presence and Shekinah	Spiritual Food Sustenance for the Journey	The Vincentian Canon Ubiquity, antiquity, universality	Eschatological Foreshadowing The Already/Not Yet	Effective Discipling Spiritual Formation in the Believing Assembly	Evangelical Witness Making Disciples of All People Groups

Appendix 6
Once upon a Time
The Cosmic Drama through a Biblical Narration of the World
Rev. Dr. Don L. Davis

From Everlasting to Everlasting, Our Lord Is God

From everlasting, in that matchless mystery of existence before time began, our Triune God dwelt in perfect splendor in eternal community as Father, Son, and Holy Spirit, the I AM, displaying his perfect attributes in eternal relationship, needing nothing, in boundless holiness, joy, and beauty. According to his sovereign will, our God purposed out of love to create a universe where his splendor would be revealed, and a world where his glory would be displayed and where a people made in his own image would dwell, sharing in fellowship with him and enjoying union with himself in relationship, all for his glory.

Who, as the Sovereign God, Created a World That Would Ultimately Rebel against His Rule

Inflamed by lust, greed, and pride, the first human pair rebelled against his will, deceived by the great prince, Satan, whose diabolical plot to supplant God as ruler of all resulted in countless angelic beings resisting God's divine will in the heavenlies. Through Adam and Eve's disobedience, they exposed themselves and their heirs to misery and death, and through their rebellion ushered creation into chaos, suffering, and evil. Through sin and rebellion, the union between God and creation was lost, and now all things are subject to the effects of this great fall – alienation, separation, and condemnation become the underlying reality for all things. No angel, human being, or creature can solve this dilemma, and without God's direct intervention, all the universe, the world, and all its creatures would be lost.

Yet, in Mercy and Loving-kindness, the Lord God Promised to Send a Savior to Redeem His Creation

In sovereign covenantal love, God determined to remedy the effects of the universe's rebellion by sending a Champion, his only Son, who would take on the form of the fallen pair, embrace and overthrow their separation from God, and suffer in the place of all humankind for its sin and disobedience. So, through his covenant faithfulness, God became directly involved in human history for the sake of their salvation. The Lord God stoops to engage his creation

Once upon a Time, continued

for the sake of restoring it, to put down evil once and for all, and to establish a people out of which his Champion would come to establish his reign in this world once more.

So, He Raised Up a People from Which the Governor Would Come
And so, through Noah, he saves the world from its own evil, through Abraham, he selects the clan through which the seed would come. Through Isaac, he continues the promise to Abraham, and through Jacob (Israel) he establishes his nation, identifying the tribe out of which he will come (Judah). Through Moses, he delivers his own from oppression and gives them his covenantal law, and through Joshua, he brings his people into the land of promise. Through judges and leaders he superintends his people, and through David, he covenants to bring a King from his clan who will reign forever. Despite his promise, though, his people fall short of his covenant time after time. Their stubborn and persistent rejection of the Lord finally leads to the nation's judgment, invasion, overthrow, and captivity. Mercifully, he remembers his covenant and allows a remnant to return – for the promise and the story were not done.

Who, as Champion, Came Down from Heaven, in the Fullness of Time, and Won through the Cross
Some four hundred years of silence occurred. Yet, in the fullness of time, God fulfilled his covenant promise by entering into this realm of evil, suffering, and alienation through the incarnation. In the person of Jesus of Nazareth, God came down from heaven and lived among us, displaying the Father's glory, fulfilling the requirements of God's moral law, and demonstrating the power of the Kingdom of God in his words, works, and exorcisms. On the Cross he took on our rebellion, destroyed death, overcame the devil, and rose on the third day to restore creation from the Fall, to make an end of sin, disease, and war, and to grant never-ending life to all people who embrace his salvation.

And, Soon and Very Soon, He Will Return to This World and Make All Things New
Ascended to the Father's right hand, the Lord Jesus Christ has sent the Holy Spirit into the world, forming a new people made up of both Jew and Gentile, the Church. Commissioned under his headship, they testify in word and deed the gospel of reconciliation to the whole creation, and when they have completed their task, he will return in glory and complete his work for creation and all

Once upon a Time, continued

creatures. Soon, he will put down sin, evil, death, and the effects of the Curse forever, and restore all creation under its true rule, refreshing all things in a new heavens and new earth, where all beings and all creation will enjoy the shalom of the Triune God forever, to his glory and honor alone.

And the Redeemed Shall Live Happily Ever After . . .

The End

Appendix 7
The Theology of Christus Victor
Rev. Dr. Don L. Davis

	The Promised Messiah	The Word Made Flesh	The Son of Man	The Suffering Servant	The Lamb of God	The Victorious Conqueror	The Reigning Lord in Heaven	The Bridegroom and Coming King
Biblical Framework	Israel's hope of Yahweh's anointed who would redeem his people	In the person of Jesus of Nazareth, the Lord has come to the world	As the promised king and divine Son of Man, Jesus reveals the Father's glory and salvation to the world	As Inaugurator of the Kingdom of God, Jesus demonstrates God's reign present through his words, wonders, and works	As both High Priest and Paschal Lamb, Jesus offers himself to God on our behalf as a sacrifice for sin	In his resurrection from the dead and ascension to God's right hand, Jesus is proclaimed as Victor over the power of sin and death	Now reigning at God's right hand till his enemies are made his footstool, Jesus pours out his benefits on his body	Soon the risen and ascended Lord will return to gather his Bride, the Church, and consummate his work
Scripture References	Isa. 9.6-7 Jer. 23.5-6 Isa. 11.1-10	John 1.14-18 Matt. 1.20-23 Phil. 2.6-8	Matt. 2.1-11 Num. 24.17 Luke 1.78-79	Mark 1.14-15 Matt. 12.25-30 Luke 17.20-21	2 Cor. 5.18-21 Isa. 52-53 John 1.29	Eph. 1.16-23 Phil. 2.5-11 Col. 1.15-20	1 Cor. 15.25 Eph. 4.15-16 Acts. 2.32-36	Rom. 14.7-9 Rev. 5.9-13 1 Thess. 4.13-18
Jesus' History	The pre-incarnate, only begotten Son of God in glory	His conception by the Spirit, and birth to Mary	His manifestation to the Magi and to the world	His teaching, exorcisms, miracles, and mighty works among the people	His suffering, crucifixion, death, and burial	His resurrection, with appearances to his witnesses, and his ascension to the Father	The sending of the Holy Spirit and his gifts, and Christ's session in heaven at the Father's right hand	His soon return from heaven to earth as Lord and Christ: the Second Coming
Description	The biblical promise for the seed of Abraham, the prophet like Moses, the son of David	In the Incarnation, God has come to us; Jesus reveals to humankind the Father's glory in fullness	In Jesus, God has shown his salvation to the entire world, including the Gentiles	In Jesus, the promised Kingdom of God has come visibly to earth, demonstrating his binding of Satan and rescinding the Curse	As God's perfect Lamb, Jesus offers himself up to God as a sin offering on behalf of the entire world	In his resurrection and ascension, Jesus destroyed death, disarmed Satan, and rescinded the Curse	Jesus is installed at the Father's right hand as Head of the Church, Firstborn from the dead, and supreme Lord in heaven	As we labor in his harvest field in the world, so we await Christ's return, the fulfillment of his promise
Church Year	Advent	Christmas	Season after Epiphany Baptism and Transfiguration	Lent	Holy Week Passion	Eastertide Easter, Ascension Day, Pentecost	Season after Pentecost Trinity Sunday	Season after Pentecost All Saints Day, Reign of Christ the King
	The Coming of Christ	The Birth of Christ	The Manifestation of Christ	The Ministry of Christ	The Suffering and Death of Christ	The Resurrection and Ascension of Christ	The Heavenly Session of Christ	The Reign of Christ
Spiritual Formation	As we await his Coming, let us proclaim and affirm the hope of Christ	O Word made flesh, let us every heart prepare him room to dwell	Divine Son of Man, show the nations your salvation and glory	In the person of Christ, the power of the reign of God has come to earth and to the Church	May those who share the Lord's death be resurrected with him	Let us participate by faith in the victory of Christ over the power of sin, Satan, and death	Come, indwell us, Holy Spirit, and empower us to advance Christ's Kingdom in the world	We live and work in expectation of his soon return, seeking to please him in all things

Appendix 8
Christus Victor: An Integrated Vision for the Christian Life
Rev. Dr. Don L. Davis

For the Church
- The Church is the primary extension of Jesus in the world
- Ransomed treasure of the victorious, risen Christ
- *Laos:* The people of God
- God's new creation: presence of the future
- Locus and agent of the Already/Not Yet Kingdom

For Theology and Doctrine
- The authoritative Word of Christ's victory: the Apostolic Tradition: the Holy Scriptures
- Theology as commentary on the grand narrative of God
- *Christus Victor* as core theological framework for meaning in the world
- The Nicene Creed: the Story of God's triumphant grace

For Spirituality
- The Holy Spirit's presence and power in the midst of God's people
- Sharing in the disciplines of the Spirit
- Gatherings, lectionary, liturgy, and our observances in the Church Year
- Living the life of the risen Christ in the rhythm of our ordinary lives

For Gifts
- God's gracious endowments and benefits from *Christus Victor*
- Pastoral offices to the Church
- The Holy Spirit's sovereign dispensing of the gifts
- Stewardship: divine, diverse gifts for the common good

Christus Victor
*Destroyer of Evil and Death
Restorer of Creation
Victor o'er Hades and Sin
Crusher of Satan*

For Worship
- People of the Resurrection: unending celebration of the people of God
- Remembering, participating in the Christ event in our worship
- Listen and respond to the Word
- Transformed at the Table, the Lord's Supper
- The presence of the Father through the Son in the Spirit

For Evangelism and Mission
- Evangelism as unashamed declaration and demonstration of *Christus Victor* to the world
- The Gospel as Good News of kingdom pledge
- We proclaim God's Kingdom come in the person of Jesus of Nazareth
- The Great Commission: go to all people groups making disciples of Christ and his Kingdom
- Proclaiming Christ as Lord and Messiah

For Justice and Compassion
- The gracious and generous expressions of Jesus through the Church
- The Church displays the very life of the Kingdom
- The Church demonstrates the very life of the Kingdom of heaven right here and now
- Having freely received, we freely give (no sense of merit or pride)
- Justice as tangible evidence of the Kingdom come

Appendix 9
Old Testament Witness to Christ and His Kingdom

Rev. Dr. Don L. Davis

Christ Is Seen in the OT's:	Covenant Promise and Fulfillment	Moral Law	Christophanies	Typology	Tabernacle, Festival, and Levitical Priesthood	Messianic Prophecy	Salvation Promises
Passage	Gen. 12.1-3	Matt. 5.17-18	John 1.18	1 Cor. 15.45	Heb. 8.1-6	Mic. 5.2	Isa. 9.6-7
Example	The Promised Seed of the Abrahamic covenant	The Law given on Mount Sinai	Commander of the Lord's army	Jonah and the great fish	Melchizedek, as both High Priest and King	The Lord's Suffering Servant	Righteous Branch of David
Christ As	Seed of the woman	The Prophet of God	God's present Revelation	Antitype of God's drama	Our eternal High Priest	The coming Son of Man	Israel's Redeemer and King
Where Illustrated	Galatians	Matthew	John	Matthew	Hebrews	Luke and Acts	John and Revelation
Exegetical Goal	To see Christ as heart of God's sacred drama	To see Christ as fulfillment of the Law	To see Christ as God's revealer	To see Christ as antitype of divine typos	To see Christ in the Temple *cultus*	To see Christ as true Messiah	To see Christ as coming King
How Seen in the NT	As fulfillment of God's sacred oath	As *telos* of the Law	As full, final, and superior revelation	As substance behind the historical shadows	As reality behind the rules and roles	As the Kingdom made present	As the One who will rule on David's throne
Our Response in Worship	God's veracity and faithfulness	God's perfect righteousness	God's presence among us	God's inspired Scripture	God's ontology: his realm as primary and determinative	God's anointed servant and mediator	God's resolve to restore his kingdom authority
How God Is Vindicated	God does not lie: he's true to his word	Jesus fulfills all righteousness	God's fulness is revealed to us in Jesus of Nazareth	The Spirit spoke by the prophets	The Lord has provided a mediator for humankind	Every jot and tittle written of him will occur	Evil will be put down, creation restored, under his reign

Appendix 10
Summary Outline of the Scriptures
Rev. Dr. Don L. Davis

The Old Testament

1. **Genesis** – *Beginnings*
   a. Adam
   b. Noah
   c. Abraham
   d. Isaac
   e. Jacob
   f. Joseph

2. **Exodus** – *Redemption (out of)*
   a. Slavery
   b. Deliverance
   c. Law
   d. Tabernacle

3. **Leviticus** – *Worship and Fellowship*
   a. Offerings and sacrifices
   b. Priests
   c. Feasts and festivals

4. **Numbers** – *Service and Walk*
   a. Organized
   b. Wanderings

5. **Deuteronomy** – *Obedience*
   a. Moses reviews history and law
   b. Civil and social laws
   c. Palestinian Covenant
   d. Moses' blessing and death

6. **Joshua** – *Redemption (into)*
   a. Conquer the land
   b. Divide up the land
   c. Joshua's farewell

7. **Judges** – *God's Deliverance*
   a. Disobedience and judgment
   b. Israel's twelve judges
   c. Lawless conditions

8. **Ruth** – *Love*
   a. Ruth chooses
   b. Ruth works
   c. Ruth waits
   d. Ruth rewarded

9. **1 Samuel** – *Kings, Priestly Perspective*
   a. Eli
   b. Samuel
   c. Saul
   d. David

10. **2 Samuel** – *David*
    a. King of Judah (9 years - Hebron)
    b. King of all Israel (33 years - Jerusalem)

11. **1 Kings** – *Solomon's Glory, Kingdom's Decline*
    a. Solomon's glory
    b. Kingdom's decline
    c. Elijah the prophet

12. **2 Kings** – *Divided Kingdom*
    a. Elisha
    b. Israel (Northern Kingdom falls)
    c. Judah (Southern Kingdom falls)

13. **1 Chronicles** – *David's Temple Arrangements*
    a. Genealogies
    b. End of Saul's reign
    c. Reign of David
    d. Temple preparations

14. **2 Chronicles** – *Temple and Worship Abandoned*
    a. Solomon
    b. Kings of Judah

15. **Ezra** – *The Minority (Remnant)*
    a. First return from exile - Zerubbabel
    b. Second return from exile - Ezra (priest)

16. **Nehemiah** – *Rebuilding by Faith*
    a. Rebuild walls
    b. Revival
    c. Religious reform

17. **Esther** – *Female Savior*
    a. Esther
    b. Haman
    c. Mordecai
    d. Deliverance: Feast of Purim

18. **Job** – *Why the Righteous Suffer*
    a. Godly Job
    b. Satan's attack
    c. Four philosophical friends
    d. God lives

19. **Psalms** – *Prayer and Praise*
    a. Prayers of David
    b. Godly suffer; deliverance
    c. God deals with Israel
    d. Suffering of God's people - end with the Lord's reign
    e. The Word of God (Messiah's suffering and glorious return)

20. **Proverbs** – *Wisdom*
    a. Wisdom vs. folly
    b. Solomon
    c. Solomon - Hezekiah
    d. Agur
    e. Lemuel

Summary Outline of the Scriptures, continued

21. **Ecclesiastes** – *Vanity*
   a. Experimentation
   b. Observation
   c. Consideration
	31. **Obadiah** – *Edom's Destruction*
	   a. Destruction prophesied
	   b. Reasons for destruction
	   c. Israel's future blessing

22. **Song of Solomon** – *Love Story*	32. **Jonah** – *Gentile Salvation*
	   a. Jonah disobeys
	   b. Others suffer
	   c. Jonah punished
	   d. Jonah obeys; thousands saved
	   e. Jonah displeased, no love for souls

23. **Isaiah** – *The Justice (Judgment) and Grace (Comfort) of God*
   a. Prophecies of punishment
   b. History
   c. Prophecies of blessing	

24. **Jeremiah** – *Judah's Sin Leads to Babylonian Captivity*
   a. Jeremiah's call; empowered
   b. Judah condemned; predicted Babylonian captivity
   c. Restoration promised
   d. Prophesied judgment inflicted
   e. Prophecies against Gentiles
   f. Summary of Judah's captivity
	33. **Micah** – *Israel's Sins, Judgment, and Restoration*
	   a. Sin and judgment
	   b. Grace and future restoration
	   c. Appeal and petition

	34. **Nahum** – *Nineveh Condemned*
	   a. God hates sin
	   b. Nineveh's doom prophesied
	   c. Reasons for doom

25. **Lamentations** – *Lament over Jerusalem*
   a. Affliction of Jerusalem
   b. Destroyed because of sin
   c. The prophet's suffering
   d. Present desolation vs. past splendor
   e. Appeal to God for mercy
	35. **Habakkuk** – *The Just Shall Live by Faith*
	   a. Complaint of Judah's unjudged sin
	   b. Chaldeans will punish
	   c. Complaint of Chaldeans' wickedness
	   d. Punishment promised
	   e. Prayer for revival; faith in God

26. **Ezekiel** – *Israel's Captivity and Restoration*
   a. Judgment on Judah and Jerusalem
   b. Judgment on Gentile nations
   c. Israel restored; Jerusalem's future glory
	36. **Zephaniah** – *Babylonian Invasion Prefigures the Day of the Lord*
	   a. Judgment on Judah foreshadows the Great Day of the Lord
	   b. Judgment on Jerusalem and neighbors foreshadows final judgment of all nations
	   c. Israel restored after judgments

27. **Daniel** – *The Time of the Gentiles*
   a. History; Nebuchadnezzar, Belshazzar, Daniel
   b. Prophecy	

28. **Hosea** – *Unfaithfulness*
   a. Unfaithfulness
   b. Punishment
   c. Restoration
	37. **Haggai** – *Rebuild the Temple*
	   a. Negligence
	   b. Courage
	   c. Separation
	   d. Judgment

29. **Joel** – *The Day of the Lord*
   a. Locust plague
   b. Events of the future Day of the Lord
   c. Order of the future Day of the Lord
	38. **Zechariah** – *Two Comings of Christ*
	   a. Zechariah's vision
	   b. Bethel's question; Jehovah's answer
	   c. Nation's downfall and salvation

30. **Amos** – *God Judges Sin*
   a. Neighbors judged
   b. Israel judged
   c. Visions of future judgment
   d. Israel's past judgment blessings
	39. **Malachi** – *Neglect*
	   a. The priest's sins
	   b. The people's sins
	   c. The faithful few

Summary Outline of the Scriptures, continued

The New Testament

1. **Matthew** – *Jesus the King*
   a. The Person of the King
   b. The Preparation of the King
   c. The Propaganda of the King
   d. The Program of the King
   e. The Passion of the King
   f. The Power of the King

2. **Mark** – *Jesus the Servant*
   a. John introduces the Servant
   b. God the Father identifies the Servant
   c. The temptation initiates the Servant
   d. Work and word of the Servant
   e. Death burial, resurrection

3. **Luke** – *Jesus Christ the Perfect Man*
   a. Birth and family of the Perfect Man
   b. Testing of the Perfect Man; hometown
   c. Ministry of the Perfect Man
   d. Betrayal, trial, and death of the Perfect Man
   e. Resurrection of the Perfect Man

4. **John** – *Jesus Christ is God*
   a. Prologue - the Incarnation
   b. Introduction
   c. Witness of works and words
   d. Witness of Jesus to his apostles
   e. Passion - witness to the world
   f. Epilogue

5. **Acts** – *The Holy Spirit Working in the Church*
   a. The Lord Jesus at work by the Holy Spirit through the apostles at Jerusalem
   b. In Judea and Samaria
   c. To the uttermost parts of the Earth

6. **Romans** – *The Righteousness of God*
   a. Salutation
   b. Sin and salvation
   c. Sanctification
   d. Struggle
   e. Spirit-filled living
   f. Security of salvation
   g. Segregation
   h. Sacrifice and service
   i. Separation and salutation

7. **1 Corinthians** – *The Lordship of Christ*
   a. Salutation and thanksgiving
   b. Conditions in the Corinthian body
   c. Concerning the Gospel
   d. Concerning collections

8. **2 Corinthians** – *The Ministry of the Church*
   a. The comfort of God
   b. Collection for the poor
   c. Calling of the Apostle Paul

9. **Galatians** – *Justification by Faith*
   a. Introduction
   b. Personal - Authority of the apostle and glory of the Gospel
   c. Doctrinal - Justification by faith
   d. Practical - Sanctification by the Holy Spirit
   e. Autographed conclusion and exhortation

10. **Ephesians** – *The Church of Jesus Christ*
    a. Doctrinal - the heavenly calling of the Church
       - A Body
       - A Temple
       - A Mystery
    b. Practical - the earthly conduct of the Church
       - A New Man
       - A Bride
       - An Army

11. **Philippians** – *Joy in the Christian Life*
    a. Philosophy for Christian living
    b. Pattern for Christian living
    c. Prize for Christian living
    d. Power for Christian living

12. **Colossians** – *Christ the Fullness of God*
    a. Doctrinal - Christ, the fullness of God; in Christ believers are made full
    b. Practical - Christ, the fullness of God; Christ's life poured out in believers, and through them

13. **1 Thessalonians** – *The Second Coming of Christ:*
    a. Is an inspiring hope
    b. Is a working hope
    c. Is a purifying hope
    d. Is a comforting hope
    e. Is a rousing, stimulating hope

14. **2 Thessalonians** – *The Second Coming of Christ*
    a. Persecution of believers now; judgment of unbelievers hereafter (at coming of Christ)
    b. Program of the world in connection with the coming of Christ
    c. Practical issues associated with the coming of Christ

Summary Outline of the Scriptures, continued

15. **1 Timothy** – *Government and Order in the Local Church*
    a. The faith of the Church
    b. Public prayer and women's place in the Church
    c. Officers in the Church
    d. Apostasy in the Church
    e. Duties of the officer of the Church

16. **2 Timothy** – *Loyalty in the Days of Apostasy*
    a. Afflictions of the Gospel
    b. Active in service
    c. Apostasy coming; authority of the Scriptures
    d. Allegiance to the Lord

17. **Titus** – *The Ideal New Testament Church*
    a. The Church is an organization
    b. The Church is to teach and preach the Word of God
    c. The Church is to perform good works

18. **Philemon** – *Reveal Christ's Love and Teach Brotherly Love*
    a. Genial greeting to Philemon and family
    b. Good reputation of Philemon
    c. Gracious plea for Onesimus
    d. Guiltless substitutes for guilty
    e. Glorious illustration of imputation
    f. General and personal requests

19. **Hebrews** – *The Superiority of Christ*
    a. Doctrinal - Christ is better than the Old Testament economy
    b. Practical - Christ brings better benefits and duties

20. **James** – *Ethics of Christianity*
    a. Faith tested
    b. Difficulty of controlling the tongue
    c. Warning against worldliness
    d. Admonitions in view of the Lord's coming

21. **1 Peter** – *Christian Hope in the Time of Persecution and Trial*
    a. Suffering and security of believers
    b. Suffering and the Scriptures
    c. Suffering and the sufferings of Christ
    d. Suffering and the Second Coming of Christ

22. **2 Peter** – *Warning against False Teachers*
    a. Addition of Christian graces gives assurance
    b. Authority of the Scriptures
    c. Apostasy brought in by false testimony
    d. Attitude toward return of Christ: test for apostasy
    e. Agenda of God in the world
    f. Admonition to believers

23. **1 John** – *The Family of God*
    a. God is light
    b. God is love
    c. God is life

24. **2 John** – *Warning against Receiving Deceivers*
    a. Walk in truth
    b. Love one another
    c. Receive not deceivers
    d. Find joy in fellowship

25. **3 John** – *Admonition to Receive True Believers*
    a. Gaius, brother in the Church
    b. Diotrephes
    c. Demetrius

26. **Jude** – *Contending for the Faith*
    a. Occasion of the epistle
    b. Occurrences of apostasy
    c. Occupation of believers in the days of apostasy

27. **Revelation** – *The Unveiling of Christ Glorified*
    a. The person of Christ in glory
    b. The possession of Jesus Christ - the Church in the World
    c. The program of Jesus Christ - the scene in Heaven
    d. The seven seals
    e. The seven trumpets
    f. Important persons in the last days
    g. The seven vials
    h. The fall of Babylon
    i. The eternal state

Appendix 11
From Before to Beyond Time
The Plan of God and Human History
Adapted from Suzanne de Dietrich. *God's Unfolding Purpose*. Philadelphia: Westminster Press, 1976.

I. Before Time (Eternity Past)

1 Cor. 2.7 – But we impart a secret and hidden wisdom of God, which God decreed before the ages for our glory (cf. Titus 1.2).

  A. The Eternal Triune God
  B. God's Eternal Purpose
  C. The Mystery of Iniquity
  D. The Principalities and Powers

II. Beginning of Time (Creation and Fall)

Gen. 1.1 – In the beginning, God created the heavens and the earth.

  A. Creative Word
  B. Humanity
  C. Fall
  D. Reign of Death and First Signs of Grace

III. Unfolding of Time (God's Plan Revealed through Israel)

Gal. 3.8 – And the Scripture, foreseeing that God would justify the Gentiles by faith, preached the Gospel beforehand to Abraham, saying, "In you shall all the nations be blessed" (cf. Rom. 9.4-5).

  A. Promise (Patriarchs)
  B. Exodus and Covenant at Sinai
  C. Promised Land
  D. The City, the Temple, and the Throne (Prophet, Priest, and King)
  E. Exile
  F. Remnant

From Before to Beyond Time, continued

IV. Fullness of Time (Incarnation of the Messiah)

Gal. 4.4-5 – But when the fullness of time had come, God sent forth his Son, born of woman, born under the law, to redeem those who were under the law, so that we might receive adoption as sons.

A. The King Comes to His Kingdom
B. The Present Reality of His Reign
C. The Secret of the Kingdom: the Already and the Not Yet
D. The Crucified King
E. The Risen Lord

V. The Last Times (The Descent of the Holy Spirit)

Acts 2.16-18 – But this is what was uttered through the prophet Joel: "'And in the last days it shall be,' God declares, 'that I will pour out my Spirit on all flesh, and your sons and your daughters shall prophesy, and your young men shall see visions, and your old men shall dream dreams; even on my male servants and female servants in those days I will pour out my Spirit, and they shall prophesy.'"

A. Between the Times: the Church as Foretaste of the Kingdom
B. The Church as Agent of the Kingdom
C. The Conflict Between the Kingdoms of Darkness and Light

VI. The Fulfillment of Time (The Second Coming)

Matt. 13.40-43 – Just as the weeds are gathered and burned with fire, so will it be at the close of the age. The Son of Man will send his angels, and they will gather out of his Kingdom all causes of sin and all lawbreakers, and throw them into the fiery furnace. In that place there will be weeping and gnashing of teeth. Then the righteous will shine like the sun in the Kingdom of their Father. He who has ears, let him hear.

A. The Return of Christ
B. Judgment
C. The Consummation of His Kingdom

From Before to Beyond Time, continued

VII. Beyond Time (Eternity Future)

1 Cor. 15.24-28 – Then comes the end, when he delivers the Kingdom to God the Father after destroying every rule and every authority and power. For he must reign until he has put all his enemies under his feet. The last enemy to be destroyed is death. For "God has put all things in subjection under his feet." But when it says, "all things are put in subjection," it is plain that he is excepted who put all things in subjection under him. When all things are subjected to him, then the Son himself will also be subjected to him who put all things in subjection under him, that God may be all in all.

A. Kingdom Handed Over to God the Father
B. God as All in All

Appendix 12
There Is a River
Identifying the Streams of a Revitalized Christian Community in the City*
Rev. Dr. Don L. Davis

Ps. 46.4 (ESV) - There is a river whose streams make glad the city of God, the holy habitation of the Most High.

		Tributaries of Authentic Historic Biblical Faith		
Recognized Biblical Identity	**Messianic Kingdom Identity**	**Revived Urban Spirituality**	**Reaffirmed Historical Connectivity**	**Refocused Kingdom Authority**
The Church Is One		*The Church Is Holy*	*The Church Is Catholic*	*The Church Is Apostolic*
A Call to Biblical Fidelity — Recognizing the Scriptures as the anchor and foundation of the Christian faith and practice		A Call to the Freedom, Power, and Fullness of the Holy Spirit — Walking in the holiness, power, gifting, and liberty of the Holy Spirit in the body of Christ	A Call to Historic Roots and Continuity — Confessing the common historical identity and continuity of authentic Christian faith	A Call to the Apostolic Faith — Affirming the apostolic tradition as the authoritative ground of the Christian hope
A Call to Messianic Kingdom Identity — Rediscovering the story of the promised Messiah and his Kingdom in Jesus of Nazareth		A Call to Live as Sojourners and Aliens as the People of God — Defining authentic Christian discipleship as faithful membership among God's people	A Call to Affirm and Express the Global Communion of Saints — Expressing cooperation and collaboration with all other believers, both local and global	A Call to Representative Authority — Submitting joyfully to God's gifted servants in the Church as undershepherds of true faith
A Call to Creedal Affinity — Embracing the Nicene Creed as the shared rule of faith of historic orthodoxy		A Call to Liturgical, Sacramental, and Catechetical Vitality — Walking in the holiness, power, gifting, and liberty of the Holy Spirit in the body of Christ	A Call to Radical Hospitality and Good Works — Expressing kingdom love to all, and especially to those of the household of faith	A Call to Prophetic and Holistic Witness — Proclaiming Christ and his Kingdom in word and deed to our neighbors and all peoples

* This schema is an adaptation and is based on the insights of the *Chicago Call* statement of May 1977, where various leading evangelical scholars and practitioners met to discuss the relationship of modern evangelicalism to the historic Christian faith.

Appendix 13

A Schematic for a Theology of the Kingdom of God

Rev. Dr. Don L. Davis

The Father Love - 1 John 4.8 Maker of heaven and earth and of all things visible and invisible.	The Son Faith - Heb. 12.2 Prophet, Priest, and King	The Spirit Hope - Rom. 15.13 Lord of the Church
Creation The triune God, Yahweh Almighty, is the Creator of all things, the Maker of the universe.	**Kingdom** The Reign of God expressed in the rule of his son Jesus the Messiah.	**Church** The Holy Spirit now indwells the one, holy, catholic, and apostolic community of Christ, which functions as a witness to (Acts 28.31) and a foretaste of (Col. 1.12; James 1.18; 1 Pet. 2.9; Rev. 1.6) the everlasting Kingdom of God.
The eternal God, Yahweh Almighty, is the triune Lord of all, Father, Son, and Holy Spirit, who is sovereign in power, infinite in wisdom, perfect in holiness, and steadfast in love. All things are from him, and through him, and to him as the source and goal of all things. O, the depth of the riches and wisdom and knowledge of God! How unsearchable are his judgments, and how inscrutable his ways! For who has known the mind of the Lord, or who has been his counselor? Or who has ever given a gift to him, that he might be repaid?" For from him and through him and to him are all things. To him be glory forever! Amen! - Rom. 11.33-36 (ESV) (cf. 1 Cor. 15.23-28; Rev. 21.1-5)	**Freedom** (Through the fall, the Slavery of Satan and sin now controls creation and all the creatures of the world. Christ has brought freedom and release through his matchless work on the Cross and the Resurrection, Rom. 8.18-21) Jesus answered them, "Truly, truly, I say to you, everyone who commits sin is a slave to sin. The slave does not remain in the house forever; the son remains forever. So if the Son sets you free, you will be free indeed." - John 8.34-36 (ESV) **Wholeness** (Through the Fall, Sickness [dis-ease] has come into the world. Christ has become our healing and immortality through the Gospel, Rev. 21.1-5]) But he was wounded for our transgressions; he was crushed for our iniquities; upon him was the chastisement that brought us peace, and with his stripes we are healed. - Isa. 53.5 (ESV) **Justice** (Through the Fall, Selfishness now dominates the relationships of the world. Christ has brought his own justice and righteousness to the Kingdom, Isa. 11.6-9!) Behold, my servant whom I have chosen, my beloved with whom my soul is well pleased. I will put my Spirit upon him, and he will proclaim justice to the Gentiles. He will not quarrel or cry aloud, nor will anyone hear his voice in the streets; a bruised reed he will not break, and a smoldering wick he will not quench, until he brings justice to victory. - Matt. 12.18-20 (ESV)	*The Church Is a Catholic (universal), Apostolic Community Where the Word Is **Rightly Preached**. Therefore It Is a Community of:* **Calling** - For freedom Christ has set us free; stand firm therefore, and do not submit again to a yoke of slavery. - Gal. 5.1 (ESV) (cf. Rom. 8.28-30; 1 Cor. 1.26-31; Eph. 1.18; 2 Thess. 2.13-14; Jude 1.1) **Faith** - ". . . for unless you believe that I am he you will die in your sins". . . . So Jesus said to the Jews who had believed in him, "If you abide in my word, you are truly my disciples, and you will know the truth, and the truth will set you free." - John 8.24b, 31-32 (ESV) (cf. Ps. 119.45; Rom. 1.17; 5.1-2; Eph. 2.8-9; 2 Tim. 1.13-14; Heb. 2.14-15; James 1.25) **Witness** - The Spirit of the Lord is upon me, because he has anointed me to proclaim good news to the poor. He has sent me to proclaim liberty to the captives and recovering of sight to the blind, to set at liberty those who are oppressed, to proclaim the year of the Lord's favor. - Luke 4.18-19 (ESV) (cf. Lev. 25.10; Prov. 31.8; Matt. 4.17; 28.18-20; Mark 13.10; Acts 1.8; 8.4, 12; 13.1-3; 25.20; 28.30-31) *The Church Is One Community Where the Sacraments Are **Rightly Administered**. Therefore It Is a Community of:* **Worship** - You shall serve the Lord your God, and he will bless your bread and your water, and I will take sickness away from among you. - Exod. 23.25 (ESV) (cf. Ps. 147.1-3; Heb. 12.28; Col. 3.16; Rev. 15.3-4; 19.5) **Covenant** - And the Holy Spirit also bears witness to us; for after the saying, "This is the covenant that I will make with them after those days, declares the Lord: I will put my laws on their hearts, and write them on their minds," then he adds, "I will remember their sins and their lawless deeds no more." - Heb. 10.15-17 (ESV) (cf. Isa. 54.10-17; Ezek. 34.25-31; 37.26-27; Mal. 2.4-5; Luke 22.20; 2 Cor. 3.6; Col. 3.15; Heb. 8.7-13; 12.22-24; 13.20-21) **Presence** - In him you also are being built together into a dwelling place for God by his Spirit. - Eph. 2.22 (ESV) (cf. Exod. 40.34-38; Ezek. 48.35; Matt. 18.18-20) *The Church Is a Holy Community Where Discipline Is **Rightly Ordered**. Therefore It Is a Community of:* **Reconciliation** - For he himself is our peace, who has made us both one and has broken down in his flesh the dividing wall of hostility by abolishing the law of commandments and ordinances, that he might create in himself one new man in place of the two, so making peace, and might reconcile us both to God in one body through the cross, thereby killing the hostility. And he came and preached peace to you who were far off and peace to those who were near. For through him we both have access in one Spirit to the Father. - Eph. 2.14-18 (ESV) (cf. Exod. 23.4-9; Lev. 19.34; Deut. 10.18-19; Ezek. 22.29; Mic. 6.8; 2 Cor. 5.16-21) **Suffering** - Since therefore Christ suffered in the flesh, arm yourselves with the same way of thinking, for whoever has suffered in the flesh has ceased from sin, so as to live for the rest of the time in the flesh no longer for human passions but for the will of God. - 1 Pet. 4.1-2 (ESV) (cf. Luke 6.22; 10.3; Rom. 8.17; 2 Tim. 2.3; 3.12; 1 Pet. 2.20-24; Heb. 5.8; 13.11-14) **Service** - But Jesus called them to him and said, "You know that the rulers of the Gentiles lord it over them, and their great ones exercise authority over them. It shall not be so among you. But whoever would be great among you must be your servant, and whoever would be first among you must be your slave even as the Son of Man came not to be served but to serve, and to give his life as a ransom for many." - Matt. 20.25-28 (ESV) (cf. 1 John 4.16-18; Gal. 2.10)

Appendix 14
Living in the Already and the Not Yet Kingdom
Rev. Dr. Don L. Davis

The Spirit: The pledge of the inheritance (*arrabon*)
The Church: The foretaste (*aparche*) of the Kingdom
"In Christ": The rich life (*en Christos*) we share as citizens of the Kingdom

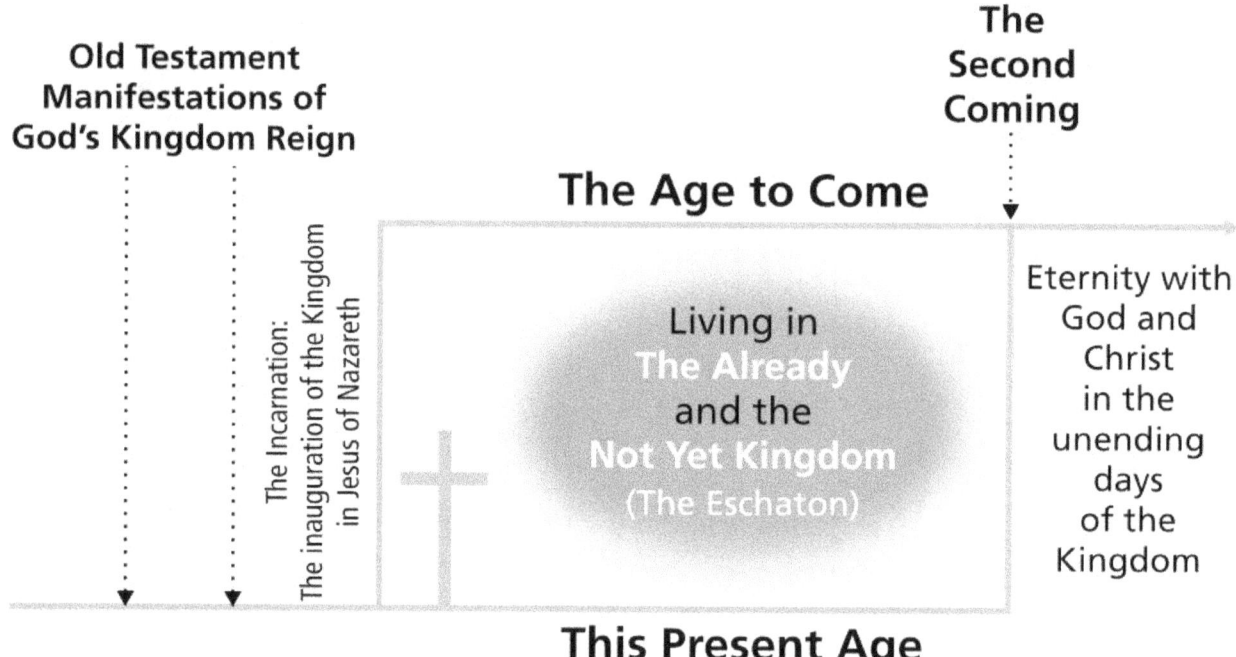

Internal enemy: The flesh (*sarx*) and the sin nature
External enemy: The world (*kosmos*) the systems of greed, lust, and pride
Infernal enemy: The devil (*kakos*) the animating spirit of falsehood and fear

Jewish View of Time

This Present Age   The Age to Come

The Coming of Messiah
The restoration of Israel
The end of Gentile oppression
The return of the earth to Edenic glory
Universal knowledge of the Lord

Appendix 15
Jesus of Nazareth: The Presence of the Future
Rev. Dr. Don L. Davis

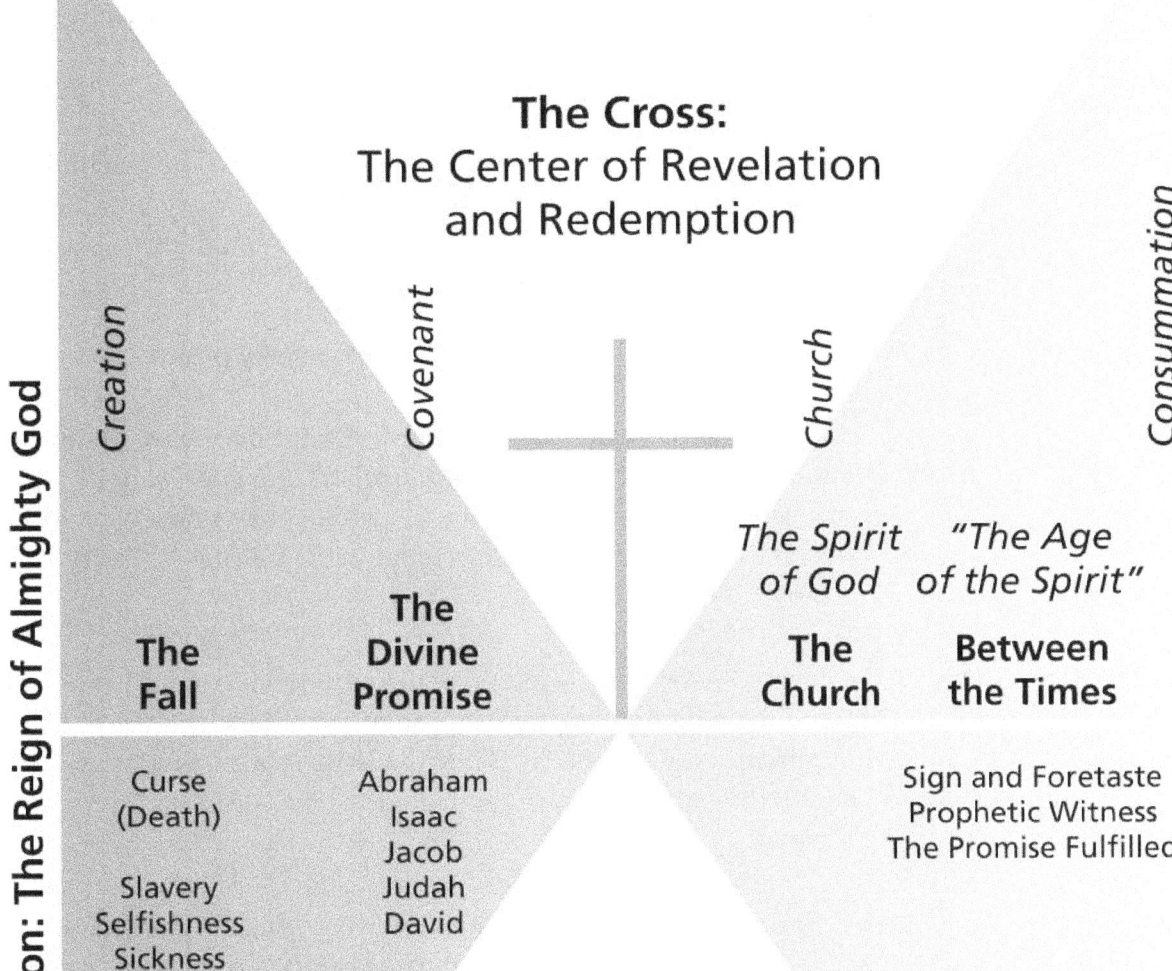

Appendix 16
Traditions (Paradosis)
Rev. Dr. Don L. Davis and Rev. Terry G. Cornett

Strong's Definition

Paradosis. Transmission, i.e. (concretely) a precept; specifically, the Jewish traditionary law

Vine's Explanation

denotes "a tradition," and hence, by metonymy, (a) "the teachings of the rabbis," . . . (b) "apostolic teaching," . . . of instructions concerning the gatherings of believers, of Christian doctrine in general . . . of instructions concerning everyday conduct.

1. **The concept of tradition in Scripture is essentially positive.**

   Jer. 6.16 (ESV) – Thus says the Lord: "Stand by the roads, and look, and ask for the ancient paths, where the good way is; and walk in it, and find rest for your souls. But they said, 'We will not walk in it'" (cf. Exod. 3.15; Judg. 2.17; 1 Kings 8.57-58; Ps. 78.1-6).

   2 Chron. 35.25 (ESV) – Jeremiah also uttered a lament for Josiah; and all the singing men and singing women have spoken of Josiah in their laments to this day. They made these a rule in Israel; behold, they are written in the Laments (cf. Gen. 32.32; Judg. 11.38-40).

   Jer. 35.14-19 (ESV) – "The command that Jonadab the son of Rechab gave to his sons, to drink no wine, has been kept, and they drink none to this day, for they have obeyed their father's command. I have spoken to you persistently, but you have not listened to me. I have sent to you all my servants the prophets, sending them persistently, saying, 'Turn now every one of you from his evil way, and amend your deeds, and do not go after other gods to serve them, and then you shall dwell in the land that I gave to you and your fathers.' But you did not incline your ear or listen to me. The sons of Jonadab the son of Rechab have kept the command that their father gave them, but this people has not obeyed me. Therefore, thus says the Lord, the God of hosts, the God of Israel: Behold, I am bringing upon Judah and all the inhabitants of Jerusalem all the disaster that I have

Traditions, continued

pronounced against them, because I have spoken to them and they have not listened, I have called to them and they have not answered." But to the house of the Rechabites Jeremiah said, "Thus says the Lord of hosts, the God of Israel: Because you have obeyed the command of Jonadab your father and kept all his precepts and done all that he commanded you, therefore thus says the Lord of hosts, the God of Israel: Jonadab the son of Rechab shall never lack a man to stand before me."

2. Godly tradition is a wonderful thing, but not all tradition is godly.

Any individual tradition must be judged by its faithfulness to the Word of God and its usefulness in helping people maintain obedience to Christ's example and teaching.¹ In the Gospels, Jesus frequently rebukes the Pharisees for establishing traditions that nullify rather than uphold God's commands.

Mark 7.8 (ESV) – You leave the commandment of God and hold to the tradition of men (cf. Matt. 15.2-6; Mark 7.13).

Col. 2.8 (ESV) – See to it that no one takes you captive by philosophy and empty deceit, according to human tradition, according to the elemental spirits of the world, and not according to Christ.

3. Without the fullness of the Holy Spirit, and the constant edification provided to us by the Word of God, tradition will inevitably lead to dead formalism.

Those who are spiritual are filled with the Holy Spirit, whose power and leading alone provides individuals and congregations a sense of freedom and vitality in all they practice and believe. However, when the practices and teachings of any given tradition are no longer infused by the power of the Holy Spirit and the Word of God, tradition loses its effectiveness, and may actually become counterproductive to our discipleship in Jesus Christ.

Eph. 5.18 (ESV) – And do not get drunk with wine, for that is debauchery, but be filled with the Spirit.

Gal. 5.22-25 (ESV) – But the fruit of the Spirit is love, joy, peace, patience, kindness, goodness, faithfulness, gentleness, self-control; against such things there is no law. And those who

---

1 "All Protestants insist that these traditions must ever be tested against Scripture and can never possess an independent apostolic authority over or alongside of Scripture." (J. Van Engen, "Tradition," *Evangelical Dictionary of Theology*, Walter Elwell, Gen. ed.) We would add that Scripture is itself the "authoritative tradition" by which all other traditions are judged. See "Appendix A, The Founders of Tradition: Three Levels of Christian Authority," at the end of this document.

Traditions, continued

belong to Christ Jesus have crucified the flesh with its passions and desires. If we live by the Spirit, let us also walk by the Spirit.

2 Cor. 3.5-6 (ESV) – Not that we are sufficient in ourselves to claim anything as coming from us, but our sufficiency is from God, who has made us competent to be ministers of a new covenant, not of the letter but of the Spirit. For the letter kills, but the Spirit gives life.

4. **Fidelity to the Apostolic Tradition (teaching and modeling) is the essence of Christian maturity.**

2 Tim. 2.2 (ESV) – and what you have heard from me in the presence of many witnesses entrust to faithful men who will be able to teach others also.

1 Cor. 11.1-2 (ESV) – Be imitators of me, as I am of Christ. Now I commend you because you remember me in everything and maintain the traditions even as I delivered them to you (cf. 1 Cor. 4.16-17, 2 Tim. 1.13-14, 2 Thess. 3.7-9, Phil. 4.9).

1 Cor. 15.3-8 (ESV) – For I delivered to you as of first importance what I also received: that Christ died for our sins in accordance with the Scriptures, that he was buried, that he was raised on the third day in accordance with the Scriptures, and that he appeared to Cephas, then to the twelve. Then he appeared to more than five hundred brothers at one time, most of whom are still alive, though some have fallen asleep. Then he appeared to James, then to all the apostles. Last of all, as to one untimely born, he appeared also to me.

5. **The Apostle Paul often includes an appeal to the tradition for support in doctrinal practices.**

1 Cor. 11.16 (ESV) – If anyone is inclined to be contentious, we have no such practice, nor do the churches of God (cf. 1 Cor. 1.2, 7.17, 15.3).

1 Cor. 14.33-34 (ESV) – For God is not a God of confusion but of peace. As in all the churches of the saints, the women should keep silent in the churches. For they are not permitted to speak, but should be in submission, as the Law also says.

Traditions, continued

6. **When a congregation uses received tradition to remain faithful to the "Word of God," they are commended by the apostles.**

   1 Cor. 11.2 (ESV) – Now I commend you because you remember me in everything and maintain the traditions even as I delivered them to you.

   2 Thess. 2.15 (ESV) – So then, brothers, stand firm and hold to the traditions that you were taught by us, either by our spoken word or by our letter.

   2 Thess. 3.6 (ESV) – Now we command you, brothers, in the name of our Lord Jesus Christ, that you keep away from any brother who is walking in idleness and not in accord with the tradition that you received from us.

Appendix A
The Founders of Tradition
Three Levels of Christian Authority

Exod. 3.15 (ESV) – God also said to Moses, "Say this to the people of Israel, 'The Lord, the God of your fathers, the God of Abraham, the God of Isaac, and the God of Jacob, has sent me to you.' This is my name forever, and thus I am to be remembered throughout all generations."

1. **The Authoritative Tradition: The Apostles and the Prophets (The Holy Scriptures)**

   Eph. 2.19-21 (ESV) – So then you are no longer strangers and aliens, but you are fellow citizens with the saints and members of the household of God, built on the foundation of the apostles and prophets, Christ Jesus himself being the cornerstone, in whom the whole structure, being joined together, grows into a holy temple in the Lord.

   ~ The Apostle Paul

   God revealed his saving work to those who would give eyewitness testimony to his glory, first in Israel, and ultimately in Jesus Christ the Messiah. This testimony is binding for all people, at all

Traditions, continued

2 See Appendix B, "Defining the Great Tradition," at the end of this document.

times, and in all places. It is the authoritative tradition by which all subsequent tradition is judged.

2. The Great Tradition: the Ecumenical Councils and their Creeds[2]

> What has been believed everywhere, always, and by all.
>
> ~ Vincent of Lerins

3 Even the more radical wing of the Protestant reformation (Anabaptists) who were the most reluctant to embrace the creeds as dogmatic instruments of faith, did not disagree with the essential content found in them. "They assumed the Apostolic Creed – they called it 'The Faith,' Der Glaube, as did most people." See John Howard Yoder, Preface to Theology: Christology and Theological Method. Grand Rapids: Brazos Press, 2002. pp. 222-223.

The Great Tradition is the core dogma (doctrine) of the Church. It represents the teaching of the Church as it has understood the Authoritative Tradition (the Holy Scriptures), and summarizes those essential truths that Christians of all ages have confessed and believed. To these doctrinal statements the whole Church (Catholic, Orthodox, and Protestant)[3] gives its assent. The worship and theology of the Church reflects this core dogma, which finds its summation and fulfillment in the person and work of Jesus Christ. From earliest times, Christians have expressed their devotion to God in its Church calendar, a yearly pattern of worship which summarizes and reenacts the events of Christ's life.

3. Specific Church Traditions: the Founders of Denominations and Orders

> The Presbyterian Church (U.S.A.) has approximately 2.5 million members, 11,200 congregations and 21,000 ordained ministers. Presbyterians trace their history to the 16th century and the Protestant Reformation. Our heritage, and much of what we believe, began with the French lawyer John Calvin (1509-1564), whose writings crystallized much of the Reformed thinking that came before him.
>
> ~ The Presbyterian Church, U.S.A.

Christians have expressed their faith in Jesus Christ in various ways through specific movements and traditions which embrace and express the Authoritative Tradition and the Great Tradition in unique ways. For instance, Catholic movements have arisen around people like Benedict, Francis, or Dominic, and among Protestants people like Martin Luther, John Calvin, Ulrich Zwingli, and John Wesley. Women have founded vital movements of Christian faith (e.g., Aimee Semple McPherson

Traditions, continued

of the Foursquare Church), as well as minorities (e.g., Richard Allen of the African Methodist Episcopal Church or Charles H. Mason of the Church of God in Christ, who also helped to spawn the Assemblies of God), all which attempted to express the Authoritative Tradition and the Great Tradition in a specific way consistent with their time and expression.

The emergence of vital, dynamic movements of the faith at different times and among different peoples reveal the fresh working of the Holy Spirit throughout history. Thus, inside Catholicism, new communities have arisen such as the Benedictines, Franciscans, and Dominicans; and outside Catholicism, new denominations have emerged (Lutherans, Presbyterians, Methodists, Church of God in Christ, etc.). Each of these specific traditions have "founders," key leaders whose energy and vision helped to establish a unique expression of Christian faith and practice. Of course, to be legitimate, these movements must adhere to and faithfully express both the Authoritative Tradition and the Great Tradition. Members of these specific traditions embrace their own practices and patterns of spirituality, but these particular features are not necessarily binding on the Church at large. They represent the unique expressions of that community's understanding of and faithfulness to the Authoritative and Great Traditions.

Specific traditions seek to express and live out this faithfulness to the Authoritative and Great Traditions through their worship, teaching, and service. They seek to make the Gospel clear within new cultures or sub-cultures, speaking and modeling the hope of Christ into new situations shaped by their own set of questions posed in light of their own unique circumstances. These movements, therefore, seek to contextualize the Authoritative tradition in a way that faithfully and effectively leads new groups of people to faith in Jesus Christ, and incorporates those who believe into the community of faith that obeys his teachings and gives witness of him to others.

Traditions, continued

Appendix B
Defining the "Great Tradition"

The Great Tradition (sometimes called the "classical Christian tradition") is defined by Robert E. Webber as follows:

> [It is] the broad outline of Christian belief and practice developed from the Scriptures between the time of Christ and the middle of the fifth century.
>
> ~ Webber. *The Majestic Tapestry.*
> Nashville: Thomas Nelson Publishers, 1986. p. 10.

This tradition is widely affirmed by Protestant theologians both ancient and modern.

> Thus those ancient Councils of Nicea, Constantinople, the first of Ephesus, Chalcedon, and the like, which were held for refuting errors, we willingly embrace, and reverence as sacred, in so far as relates to doctrines of faith, for they contain nothing but the pure and genuine interpretation of Scripture, which the holy Fathers with spiritual prudence adopted to crush the enemies of religion who had then arisen.
>
> ~ John Calvin. *Institutes.* IV, ix. 8.

> ... most of what is enduringly valuable in contemporary biblical exegesis was discovered by the fifth century.
>
> ~ Thomas C. Oden. *The Word of Life.*
> San Francisco: HarperSanFrancisco, 1989. p. xi

> The first four Councils are by far the most important, as they settled the orthodox faith on the Trinity and the Incarnation.
>
> ~ Philip Schaff. *The Creeds of Christendom.* Vol. 1.
> Grand Rapids: Baker Book House, 1996. p. 44.

Our reference to the Ecumenical Councils and Creeds is, therefore, focused on those Councils which retain a widespread agreement in the Church among Catholics, Orthodox, and Protestants. While Catholic and Orthodox share common agreement on the first seven councils, Protestants tend to affirm and use primarily the first four.

Traditions, continued

Therefore, those councils which continue to be shared by the whole Church are completed with the Council of Chalcedon in 451.

It is worth noting that each of these four Ecumenical Councils took place in a pre-European cultural context and that none of them were held in Europe. They were councils of the whole Church and they reflected a time in which Christianity was primarily an eastern religion in it's geographic core. By modern reckoning, their par- ticipants were African, Asian, and European. The councils reflected a church that ". . . has roots in cultures far distant from Europe and preceded the development of modern European identity, and [of which] some of its greatest minds have been African" (Oden, *The Living God*, San Francisco: HarperSanFrancisco, 1987, p. 9).

Perhaps the most important achievement of the Councils was the creation of what is now commonly called the Nicene Creed. It serves as a summary statement of the Christian faith that can be agreed on by Catholic, Orthodox, and Protestant Christians.

The first four Ecumenical Councils are summarized in the following chart:

Name/Date/Location	Purpose
First Ecumenical Council 325 A.D. Nicea, Asia Minor	Defending against: *Arianism* Question answered: *Was Jesus God?* Action: *Developed the initial form of the Nicene Creed to serve as a summary of the Christian faith*
Second Ecumenical Council 381 A.D. Constantinople, Asia Minor	Defending against: *Macedonianism* Question answered: *Is the Holy Spirit a personal and equal part of the Godhead?* Action: *Completed the Nicene Creed by expanding the article dealing with the Holy Spirit*
Third Ecumenical Council 431 A.D. Ephesus, Asia Minor	Defending against: *Nestorianism* Question answered: *Is Jesus Christ both God and man in one person?* Action: *Defined Christ as the Incarnate Word of God and affirmed his mother Mary as theotokos (God-bearer)*
Fourth Ecumenical Council 451 A.D. Chalcedon, Asia Minor	Defending against: *Monophysitism* Question answered: *How can Jesus be both God and man?* Action: *Explained the relationship between Jesus' two natures (human and Divine)*

Appendix 17
Documenting Your Work
A Guide to Help You Give Credit Where Credit Is Due
The Urban Ministry Institute

Avoiding Plagiarism

Plagiarism is using another person's ideas as if they belonged to you without giving them proper credit. In academic work it is just as wrong to steal a person's ideas as it is to steal a person's property. These ideas may come from the author of a book, an article you have read, or from a fellow student. The way to avoid plagiarism is to carefully use "notes" (textnotes, footnotes, endnotes, etc.) and a "Works Cited" section to help people who read your work know when an idea is one you thought of, and when you are borrowing an idea from another person.

Using Citation References

A citation reference is required in a paper whenever you use ideas or information that came from another person's work.

All citation references involve two parts:

- Notes in the body of your paper placed next to each quotation which came from an outside source.
- A "Works Cited" page at the end of your paper or project which gives information about the sources you have used

Using Notes in Your Paper

There are three basic kinds of notes: parenthetical notes, footnotes, and endnotes. At The Urban Ministry Institute, we recommend that students use parenthetical notes. These notes give the author's last name(s), the date the book was published, and the page number(s) on which you found the information. Example:

> In trying to understand the meaning of Genesis 14.1-24, it is important to recognize that in biblical stories "the place where dialogue is first introduced will be an important moment in revealing the character of the speaker . . ." (Kaiser and Silva 1994, 73). This is certainly true of the character of Melchizedek who speaks words of blessing. This identification of Melchizedek as a positive spiritual influence is reinforced by the fact that

Documenting Your Work, continued

he is the King of Salem, since Salem means "safe, at peace" (Wiseman 1996, 1045).

Creating a Works Cited Page

A "Works Cited" page should be placed at the end of your paper. This page:

- lists every source you quoted in your paper
- is in alphabetical order by author's last name
- includes the date of publication and information about the publisher

The following formatting rules should be followed:

1. Title

The title "Works Cited" should be used and centered on the first line of the page following the top margin.

2. Content

Each reference should list:
- the author's full name (last name first)
- the date of publication
- the title and any special information (Revised edition, 2nd edition, reprint) taken from the cover or title page should be noted
- the city where the publisher is headquartered followed by a colon and the name of the publisher

3. Basic form

- Each piece of information should be separated by a period.
- The second line of a reference (and all following lines) should be indented.
- Book titles should be underlined (or italicized).
- Article titles should be placed in quotes.

Documenting Your Work, continued

> **Example:**
>
> Fee, Gordon D. 1991. *Gospel and Spirit: Issues in New Testament Hermeneutics.* Peabody, MA: Hendrickson Publishers.
>
> **4. Special Forms**
>
> *A book with multiple authors:*
>
> Kaiser, Walter C., and Moisés Silva. 1994. *An Introduction to Biblical Hermeneutics: The Search for Meaning.* Grand Rapids: Zondervan Publishing House.
>
> *An edited book:*
>
> Greenway, Roger S., ed. 1992. *Discipling the City: A Comprehensive Approach to Urban Mission.* 2nd ed. Grand Rapids: Baker Book House.
>
> *A book that is part of a series:*
>
> Morris, Leon. 1971. *The Gospel According to John.* Grand Rapids: Wm. B. Eerdmans Publishing Co. The New International Commentary on the New Testament. Gen. ed. F. F. Bruce.
>
> *An article in a reference book:*
>
> Wiseman, D. J. "Salem." 1982. In *New Bible Dictionary.* Leicester, England - Downers Grove, IL: InterVarsity Press. Eds. I. H. Marshall and others.
>
> *(An example of a "Works Cited" page is located at the end of this appendix.)*
>
> **For Further Research**
>
> Standard guides to documenting academic work in the areas of philosophy, religion, theology, and ethics include:
>
> Atchert, Walter S., and Joseph Gibaldi. 1985. *The MLA Style Manual.* New York: Modern Language Association.

Documenting Your Work, continued

The Chicago Manual of Style. 1993. 14th ed. Chicago: The University of Chicago Press.

Turabian, Kate L. 1987. *A Manual for Writers of Term Papers, Theses, and Dissertations*. 5th edition. Bonnie Bertwistle Honigsblum, ed. Chicago: The University of Chicago Press.

Example of a "Works Cited" listing

Works Cited

Fee, Gordon D. 1991. *Gospel and Spirit: Issues in New Testament Hermeneutics*. Peabody, MA: Hendrickson Publishers.

Greenway, Roger S., ed. 1992. *Discipling the City: A Comprehensive Approach to Urban Mission*. 2nd ed. Grand Rapids: Baker Book House.

Kaiser, Walter C., and Moisés Silva. 1994. *An Introduction to Biblical Hermeneutics: The Search for Meaning*. Grand Rapids: Zondervan Publishing House.

Morris, Leon. 1971. *The Gospel According to John*. Grand Rapids: Wm. B. Eerdmans Publishing Co. The New International Commentary on the New Testament. Gen. ed. F. F. Bruce.

Wiseman, D. J. "Salem." 1982. In *New Bible Dictionary*. Leicester, England-Downers Grove, IL: InterVarsity Press. Eds. I. H. Marshall and others.

Appendix 18
Representin': Jesus as God's Chosen Representative
Rev. Dr. Don L. Davis

To represent another is to be selected to stand in the place of another, and thereby fulfill the assigned duties, exercise the rights and serve as deputy for, as well as to speak and act with another's authority on behalf of their interests and reputation.

The Temptation of Jesus Christ
Challenge to and Contention with God's Rep

Mark 1.12-13 – The Spirit immediately drove him out into the wilderness. [13] *And he was in the wilderness forty days, being tempted by Satan.* And he was with the wild animals, and the angels were ministering to him.

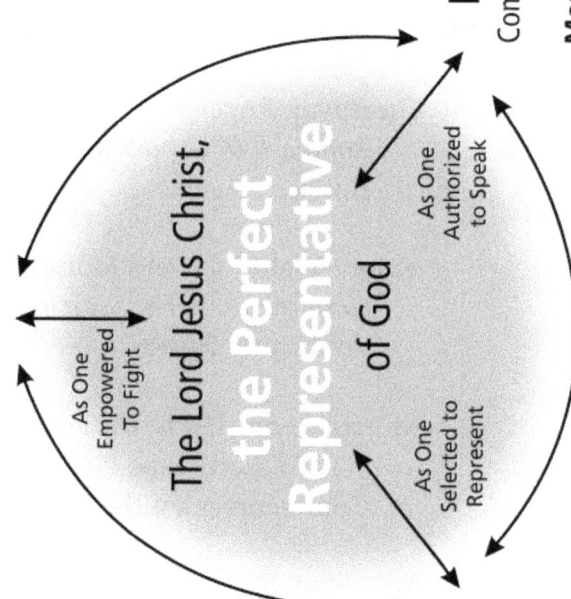

The Lord Jesus Christ, the Perfect Representative of God

- As One Empowered To Fight
- As One Authorized to Speak
- As One Selected to Represent

The Public Preaching Ministry of Jesus Christ
Communication and Conveyance by God's Rep

Mark 1.14-15 – Now after John was arrested, Jesus came into Galilee, proclaiming the gospel of God, and saying, "The time is fulfilled, and the kingdom of God is at hand; repent and believe in the gospel."

Jesus Fulfills The Duties Of Being an Emissary

1. Receiving an *Assignment*, John 10.17-18
2. Resourced with an *Entrustment*, John 3.34; Luke. 4.18
3. Launched into *Engagement*, John 5.30
4. Answered with an *Assessment*, Matthew 3.16-17
5. New assignment after Assessment, Philippians 2.9-11

The Baptism of Jesus Christ
Commissioning and Confirmation of God's Rep

Mark 1.9-11 – *In those days Jesus came from Nazareth of Galilee and was baptized by John in the Jordan.* [10] And when he came up out of the water, immediately he saw the heavens opening and the Spirit descending on him like a dove. [11] And a voice came from heaven, "You are my beloved Son; with you I am well pleased."

Appendix 19
Faithfully Re-presenting Jesus of Nazareth
Rev. Dr. Don L. Davis

Eph. 4.17-19 – Now this I say and testify in the Lord, that you must no longer walk as the Gentiles do, in the futility of their minds [18] They are darkened in their understanding, alienated from the life of God because of the ignorance that is in them, due to their hardness of heart. [19] They have become callous and have given themselves up to sensuality, greedy to practice every kind of impurity.

Eph. 4.20-23 – But that is not the way you learned Christ! - [21] assuming that you have heard about him and were taught in him, as the truth is in Jesus, [22] to put off your old self, which belongs to your former manner of life and is corrupt through deceitful desires, [23] and to be renewed in the spirit of your minds.

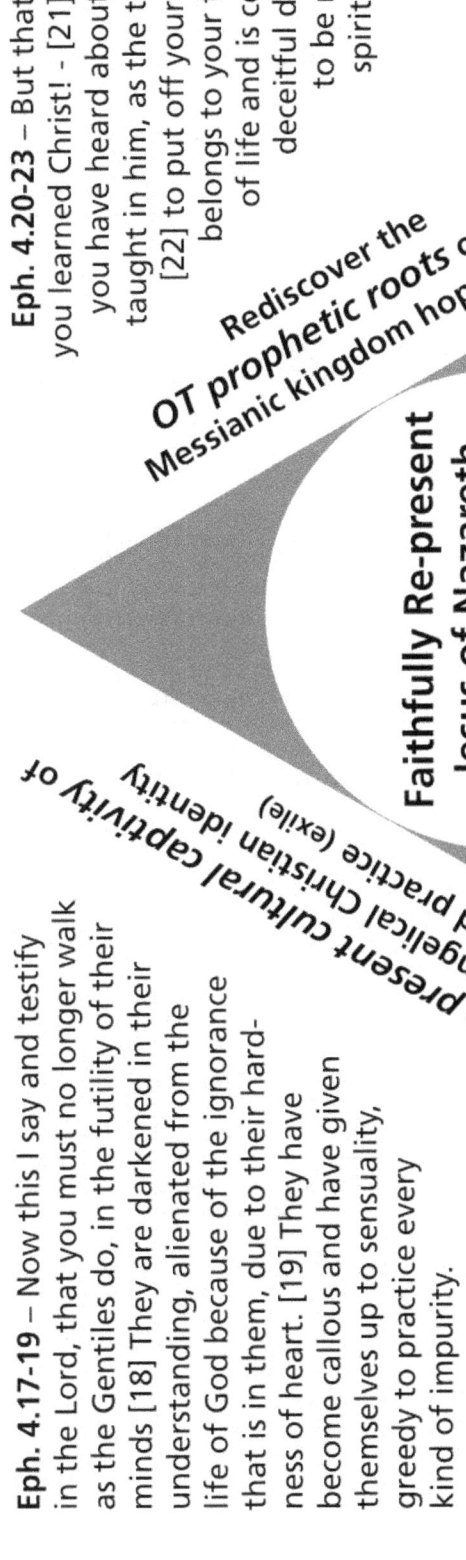

Rediscover the
OT prophetic roots of the
Messianic kingdom hope (return)

Faithfully Re-present Jesus of Nazareth

with fidelity to Holy Scripture
in sync with apostolic tradition
contextualizing biblical language
without cultural distortion

Recognize the **present cultural captivity of much evangelical Christian identity and practice** (exile)

Re-experience and embrace the power of
the NT apostolic vision and drama [myth]
(possession)

Eph. 4.24-25 – and to put on the new self, created after the likeness of God in true righteousness and holiness. [25] Therefore, having put away falsehood, let each one of you speak the truth with his neighbor, for we are members one of another.

Appendix 20
Messianic Prophecies Cited in the New Testament
Rev. Dr. Don L. Davis

	NT Citation	OT Reference	Indication of the Fulfillment of the Messianic Prophecy
1	Matt. 1.23	Isa. 7.14	The virgin birth of Jesus of Nazareth
2	Matt. 2.6	Mic. 5.2	The birth of Messiah in Bethlehem
3	Matt. 2.15	Hos. 11.1	That Yahweh would call Messiah out of Egypt, the second Israel
4	Matt. 2.18	Jer. 31.15	Rachel weeping over infants slain by Herod seeking to destroy Messianic seed
5	Matt. 3.3	Isa. 40.3	John the Baptist's preaching fulfills the Messianic forerunner of Isaiah
6	Matt. 4.15-16	Isa. 9.1-2	Galilean ministry of Jesus fulfills Isaiah's prophecy of Messiah's light to the Gentiles
7	Matt. 8.17	Isa. 53.4	Healing ministry of Jesus fulfills Isaiah's prophecy regarding Messiah's power to exorcize and heal
8	Matt. 11.14-15	Isa. 35.5-6; 61.1	Jesus' healing ministry confirms his identity as Yahweh's anointed Messiah
9	Matt. 11.10	Mal. 3.1	Jesus confirms John the Baptist's identity as the messenger of Yahweh in Malachi
10	Matt. 12.18-21	Isa. 42.1-4	Jesus' healing ministry fulfills Isaiah's prophecy of Messiah's compassion for the weak
11	Matt. 12.40	Jon. 1.17	As Jonah was three days and nights in the belly of the sea monster, so Jesus would be in the earth
12	Matt. 13.14-15	Isa. 6.9-10	The spiritual dullness of Jesus' audience
13	Matt. 13.35	Ps. 78.2	Messiah would teach in parables to the people
14	Matt. 15.8-9	Isa. 29.13	Hypocritical nature of the audience of Jesus
15	Matt. 21.5	Zech. 9.9	Triumphal entry of Messiah the King into Jerusalem upon the foal of a donkey
16	Matt. 21.9	Ps. 118.26-27	Hosannas to the King of Jerusalem
17	Matt. 21.16	Ps. 8.2	Out of the mouth of babes Yahweh declares salvation
18	Matt. 21.42	Ps. 118.22	The Stone which the builders rejected has become the Capstone
19	Matt. 23.39	Ps. 110.1	The enthronement of Yahweh's Lord
20	Matt. 24.30	Dan. 7.13	The Son of Man to come, of Daniel's prophecy, is none other than Jesus of Nazareth
21	Matt. 26.31	Zech. 13.7	The Shepherd smitten by Yahweh and the sheep scattered

Messianic Prophecies Cited in the New Testament, continued

	NT Citation	OT Reference	Indication of the Fulfillment of the Messianic Prophecy
22	Matt. 26.64	Ps. 110.1	Jesus of Nazareth is the fulfillment of Daniel's Messianic Son of Man
23	Matt. 26.64	Dan. 7.3	Jesus will come in the clouds of heaven as Daniel's exalted ruler
24	Matt. 27.9-10	Zech. 11.12-13	Messiah is betrayed for thirty pieces of silver
25	Matt. 27.34-35	Ps. 69.21	God's anointed is given wine mingled with gall
26	Matt. 27.43	Ps. 22.18	The soldiers cast lots for the garments of the Messiah
27	Matt. 27.43	Ps. 22.8	Messiah receives mockery and derision upon the cross
28	Matt. 27.46	Ps. 22.1	Messiah forsaken by God for the sake of others
29	Mark 1.2	Mal. 3.1	John the Baptist is the fulfillment of the prophecy regarding the Lord's messenger
30	Mark 1.3	Isa. 40.3	John the Baptist is the voice calling in the wilderness to prepare the Lord's way
31	Mark 4.12	Isa. 6.9	The spiritual dullness of the audience in regard to Messiah's message
32	Mark 7.6	Isa. 29.13	Hypocrisy of the audience in their response to Messiah
33	Mark 11.9	Ps. 118.25	Hosannas given to Messiah's entry as King into Jerusalem
34	Mark 12.10-11	Ps. 118.25	The stone which the builders rejected has become the chief cornerstone
35	Mark 12.36	Ps. 110.1	The Lord enthrones the Lord of David upon his throne in Zion
36	Mark 13.26	Dan. 7.13	Jesus is the prophesied Son of Man who will return in glory in the clouds
37	Mark 14.27	Zech 13.7	Jesus will be forsaken by his own, for the shepherd will be smitten and the sheep scattered
38	Mark 14.62	Dan. 7.13	Jesus is the Messiah, the Son of Man of Daniel's vision
39	Mark 14.62	Ps. 110.1	The Son of Man, who is Jesus, will come from the right hand of Yahweh
40	Mark 15.24	Ps. 22.18	Lots are cast for the garments of Messiah during his passion
41	Mark 15.34	Ps. 22.1	Messiah is forsaken by God for the redemption of the world
42	Luke 1.17	Mal. 4.6	John the Baptist will come in the power ad the spirit of Elijah
43	Luke 1.76	Mal. 3.1	John goes before the Lord to prepare the way
44	Luke 1.79	Isa. 9.1-2	Messiah will give light to those who dwell in darkness
45	Luke 2.32	Isa. 42.6; 49.6	Messiah will be a light to the Gentiles

Messianic Prophecies Cited in the New Testament, continued

	NT Citation	OT Reference	Indication of the Fulfillment of the Messianic Prophecy
46	Luke 3.4-5	Isa. 40.3	John is Isaiah's voice that cries in the wilderness to prepare the Lord's way
47	Luke 4.18-19	Isa. 61.1-2	Jesus is Yahweh's servant, anointed by his Spirit to bring the good news of the Kingdom
48	Luke 7.27	Mal. 3.1	Jesus confirms John's identity as the preparer of the Lord's way
49	Luke 8.10	Isa. 6.9	The dullness of the audience to Messiah Jesus
50	Luke 19.38	Ps. 118.26	Jesus fulfills in his entry into Jerusalem the Messianic prophecy of the King of Israel
51	Luke 20.17	Ps. 118.26	Jesus is Yahweh's stone which the builders rejected, which has become the Capstone
52	Luke 20.42-43	Ps. 110.1	David calls his lord the Messiah and Lord, who is enthroned in Zion by Yahweh
53	Luke 22.37	Isa. 53.12	Messiah is classed among criminals
54	Luke 22.69	Ps. 110.1	Jesus will return from the right hand of God, from where he has been enthroned
55	Luke 23.34	Ps. 22.18	Lots are cast for the garments of Messiah
56	John 1.23	Isa. 40.3	John's preaching is the fulfillment of Isaiah's prophecy about the forerunner of the Messiah
57	John 2.17	Ps. 69.17	Zeal for the house of the Lord will consume Messiah
58	John 6.45	Isa. 54.13	All those whom God teaches will come to Messiah
59	John 7.42	Ps. 89.4; Mic. 5.2	Messiah, the seed of David, will be from Bethlehem
60	John 12.13	Ps. 118.25-26	Hosannas are given to Israel's triumphant Messiah King
61	John 12.15	Zech 9.9	The King of Israel enters Jerusalem upon the foal of a donkey
62	John 12.38	Isa. 53.1	As Isaiah prophesied, few believed the report of Yahweh about his anointed one
63	John 12.40	Isa. 6.10	Isaiah saw the glory of Messiah and spoke of the dullness of his audience to him
64	John 13.18; cf. 17.12	Ps. 41.9	Betrayal of Messiah by one of his intimate followers
65	John 15.25	Pss. 35.19; 69.4	Messiah will be hated without cause
66	John 19.24	Ps. 22.18	The garments of Messiah will be divided
67	John 19.28	Ps. 69.21	Messiah will be offered wine upon the cross
68	John 19.36	Exod. 12.46; Num. 9.12; Ps. 34.20	Not one bone of the Messiah will be broken

Messianic Prophecies Cited in the New Testament, continued

	NT Citation	OT Reference	Indication of the Fulfillment of the Messianic Prophecy
69	John 19.37	Zech. 12.10	The repentant nation of Israel will look upon him whom they have pierced
70	Acts 1.20	Pss. 69.25; 109.8	Judas is to be replaced by another
71	Acts 2.16-21	Joel 2.28-32	The Spirit is to be poured out in the last days upon all flesh
72	Acts 2.25-28	Ps. 16.8-11	Messiah could not undergo decay or corruption in Sheol
73	Acts 2.34-35	Ps. 110.1	Messiah is enthroned at Yahweh's right hand until his enemies are defeated
74	Acts 3.22-23	Deut. 18.15, 19	God would raise up for the people a prophet like Moses
75	Acts 3.25	Gen. 22.18	All nations of the earth would be blessed in the seed of Abraham
76	Acts 4.11	Ps. 118.22	Messiah Jesus is the rejected stone whom God has made the cornerstone
77	Acts 4.25	Ps. 2.1	Yahweh will laugh at the opposition given by the nations to him and his anointed
78	Acts 7.37	Deut. 18.15	Yahweh will give to Israel a prophet like Moses
79	Acts 8.32-33	Isa. 53.7-9	Messiah Jesus is the Suffering Servant of Yahweh
80	Acts 13.33	Ps. 2.7	God has fulfilled the promise to Israel in Jesus by raising him from the dead
81	Acts 13.34	Isa. 53.3	Messiah Jesus is the fulfillment of the sure mercies of David
82	Acts 13.35	Ps. 16.10	Messiah would not undergo corruption in the grave
83	Acts 13.47	Isa. 49.6	Through Paul, the message of the Messiah becomes a light to the nations
84	Acts 15.16-18	Amos 9.11-12	The dynasty of David is restored in Jesus, and Gentiles are welcomed into the Kingdom
85	Rom. 9.25-26	Amos 9.11-12	Gentiles are to become the people of God
86	Rom. 9.33; 10.11	Isa. 28.16	Messiah becomes a stone of stumbling to those who reject God's salvation
87	Rom. 10.13	Joel 2.32	Anyone calling on the name of the Lord will be saved
88	Rom. 11.8	Isa. 29.10	Israel through unbelief has been hardened to Messiah
89	Rom. 11.9-10	Ps. 69.22-23	Judgment has hardened upon Israel
90	Rom. 11.26	Isa. 59.20-21	A deliverer will come from Zion
91	Rom. 11.27	Isa. 27.9	Forgiveness of sins will be given through a new covenant
92	Rom. 14.11	Isa. 45.23	All will be finally judged by Yahweh

Messianic Prophecies Cited in the New Testament, continued

	NT Citation	OT Reference	Indication of the Fulfillment of the Messianic Prophecy
93	Rom. 15.9	Ps. 18.49	Gentiles praise God through faith in Messiah
94	Rom. 15.10	Deut. 32.43	God receives praise from the nations
95	Rom. 15.11	Ps. 117.1	The peoples of the earth give God glory
96	Rom. 15.12	Isa. 11.10	Gentiles will hope in the root of Jesse
97	Rom. 15.21	Isa. 52.15	The Good News will be preached to those without understanding
98	1 Cor. 15.27	Ps. 8.7	All things are under the feet of God's representative head
99	1 Cor. 15.54	Isa. 25.8	Death will be swallowed up in victory
100	1 Cor. 15.55	Hos. 13.14	Death will one day lose its sting altogether
101	2 Cor. 6.2	Isa. 49.8	Now is the day of salvation through faith in Messiah Jesus
102	2 Cor. 6.16	Ezek. 37.27	God will dwell with his people
103	2 Cor. 6.18	Hos. 1.10; Isa. 43.6	Believers in Messiah Jesus are the sons and daughters of God
104	Gal. 3.8, 16	Gen. 12.3; 13.15; 17.8	The Scriptures, foreseeing Gentile justification by faith, preached the Gospel beforehand through the promise to Abraham, that all nations would be blessed in his seed
105	Gal. 4.27	Isa. 54.1	Jerusalem is the mother of us all
106	Eph. 2.17	Isa. 57.19	Peace of Messiah Jesus is preached both to the Jew and the Gentile
107	Eph. 4.8	Ps. 68.18	Messiah in his ascension has conquered and given gifts to us all by his grace
108	Eph. 5.14	Isa. 26.19; 51.17; 52.1; 60.1	The regeneration of the Lord has occurred; his light has shined on us
109	Heb. 1.5	Ps. 2.7	Messiah is God's Son
110	Heb. 1.5	2 Sam. 7.14	Messiah Jesus is the anointed Son of God
111	Heb. 1.6	Deut. 32.43	Angels worshiped Messiah when he entered the world
112	Heb. 1.8-9	Ps. 45.6-7	Messiah Jesus is referred to as God by Yahweh in direct address
113	Heb. 1.10-12	Ps. 102.25-27	The Son is the agent of God's creation and is eternal
114	Heb. 1.13	Ps. 110.1	Messiah Jesus is enthroned at the Father's right hand
115	Heb. 2.6-8	Ps. 8.4-6	All things have been made subject to the Son's authority
116	Heb. 2.12	Ps. 22.22	Messiah Jesus is a brother to all of the redeemed
117	Heb. 5.5	Isa. 8.17-18	Messiah puts his trust in Yahweh God

Messianic Prophecies Cited in the New Testament, continued

	NT Citation	OT Reference	Indication of the Fulfillment of the Messianic Prophecy
118	Heb. 5.5	Ps. 2.7	Messiah is God's Son
119	Heb. 5.6	Ps. 110.4	Messiah is an eternal priest after the order of Melchizedek
120	Heb. 7.17, 21	Ps. 110.4	Messiah Jesus is an eternal High Priest
121	Heb. 8.8-12	Jer. 31.31-34	A new covenant has been made in the blood of Jesus
122	Heb. 10.5-9	Ps. 40.6	The death of Messiah Jesus replaces the atoning system of Temple sacrifice
123	Heb. 10.13	Ps. 110.1	Yahweh has enthroned Messiah Jesus as Lord
124	Heb. 10.16-17	Jer. 31.33-34	The Holy Spirit bears witness of the sufficiency of the New Covenant
125	Heb. 10.37-38	Hab. 2.3-4	He who will come will do so, in a little while
126	Heb. 12.26	Hag. 2.6	All heaven and earth will be shaken
127	1 Pet. 2.6	Isa. 28.16	God lays a cornerstone in Zion
128	1 Pet. 2.7	Ps. 118.22	The stone which the builders rejected, God has made the Capstone
129	1 Pet. 2.8	Isa. 8.14	Messiah is a stone of stumbling to those who do not believe
130	1 Pet. 2.10	Hos. 1.10; 2.23	Gentiles through Messiah are now invited to become the people of God
131	1 Pet. 2.22	Isa. 53.9	The sinless Messiah Jesus was sacrificed for us

Appendix 21
Ethics of the New Testament:
Living in the Upside-Down Kingdom of God
Rev. Dr. Don L. Davis

The Principle of Reversal

The Principle Expressed	Scripture
The poor shall become rich, and the rich shall become poor	Luke 6.20-26
The law breaker and the undeserving are saved	Matt. 21.31-32
Those who humble themselves shall be exalted	1 Pet. 5.5-6
Those who exalt themselves shall be brought low	Luke 18.14
The blind shall be given sight	John 9.39
Those claiming to see shall be made blind	John 9.40-41
We become free by being Christ's slave	Rom. 12.1-2
God has chosen what is foolish in the world to shame the wise	1 Cor. 1.27
God has chosen what is weak in the world to shame the strong	1 Cor. 1.27
God has chosen the low and despised to bring to nothing things that are	1 Cor. 1.28
We gain the next world by losing this one	1 Tim. 6.7
Love this life and you'll lose it; hate this life, and you'll keep the next	John 12.25
You become the greatest by being the servant of all	Matt. 10.42-45
Store up treasures here, you forfeit heaven's reward	Matt. 6.19
Store up treasures above, you gain heaven's wealth	Matt. 6.20
Accept your own death to yourself in order to live fully	John 12.24
Release all earthly reputation to gain heaven's favor	Phil. 3.3-7
The first shall be last, and the last shall become first	Mark 9.35
The grace of Jesus is perfected in your weakness, not your strength	2 Cor. 12.9
God's highest sacrifice is contrition and brokenness	Ps. 51.17
It is better to give to others than to receive from them	Acts 20.35
Give away all you have in order to receive God's best	Luke 6.38

Appendix 22
Preaching and Teaching Jesus of Nazareth as Messiah and Lord Is the Heart of All Biblical Ministry

Rev. Dr. Don L. Davis

Phil. 3.8 (ESV) – Indeed, I count everything as loss because of the surpassing worth of **knowing Christ [Messiah] Jesus my Lord**. For his sake I have suffered the loss of all things and count them as rubbish, in order *that I may gain Christ [Messiah]*.

Acts 5.42 (ESV) – And every day, in the temple and from house to house, they *did not cease teaching and preaching Jesus as the Christ [Messiah]*.

1 Cor. 1.23 (ESV) – but we preach *Christ [Messiah] crucified*, a stumbling block to Jews and folly to Gentiles.

2 Cor. 4.5 (ESV) – For what we proclaim is not ourselves, but *Jesus Christ [Messiah] as Lord*, with ourselves as your servants for Jesus= sake.

1 Cor. 2.2 (ESV) – For I decided to know nothing among you except *Jesus Christ [Messiah] and him crucified*.

Eph. 3.8 (ESV) – To me, though I am the very least of all the saints, this grace was given, *to preach to the Gentiles the unsearchable riches of Christ [Messiah]*.

Phil. 1.18 (ESV) – What then? Only that in every way, whether in pretense or in truth, *Christ [Messiah] is proclaimed*, and in that I rejoice. Yes, and I will rejoice.

Col. 1.27-29 (ESV) – To them God chose to make known how great among the Gentiles are the riches of the glory of this mystery, which is *Christ [Messiah] in you, the hope of glory*. [28] Him we proclaim, warning everyone and teaching everyone with all wisdom, that we may *present everyone mature in Christ [Messiah]*. [29] For this I toil, *struggling with all his energy* that he powerfully works within me.

Appendix 23
Summary of Messianic Interpretations in the Old Testament
Rev. Dr. Don L. Davis, adapted from James Smith, *The Promised Messiah*

Legend: EJ - Early Jewish Interpretation NTA - New Testament Allusion
NTE - New Testament Exegesis CF - Church Fathers

No.	Bible Reference	Summary of the Messianic Prophecy	EJ	NTA	NTE	CF
1	Gen. 3.15	One from the ranks of the seed of the woman will crush the head of the serpent	X	X		X
2	Gen. 9.25-27	God will come and dwell in the tents of Shem	X	X		X
3	Gen. 12.3; 18.18; 22.18; 26.4; 28.14	All nations of the earth will be blessed through the seed of Abraham, Isaac, and Jacob	X	X	X	X
4	Gen. 49.10-11	The Scepter won't depart from Judah until Shiloh comes, and all the nations will be obedient to him	X	X		X
5	Num. 24.16-24	A powerful Ruler from Israel will come and crush the enemies of God's people	X	X		X
6	Deut. 18.15-18	A prophet like Moses will come and all the righteous will listen to him		X	X	X
7	Deut. 32.43	The angels of God commanded to rejoice as the Firstborn of God comes into the world		X		
8	1 Sam. 2.10	God will judge the ends of the earth but will give strength to his anointed	X			X
9	1 Sam. 2.35-36	A faithful Priest will come and dispense blessing upon the people				
10	2 Sam. 7.12-16	The Seed of David will sit upon an eternal throne, and will build the house of God		X		X
11	Ps. 89	God's covenant to send Messiah through David cannot be revoked	X			
12	Ps. 132	God has chosen David and Zion		X		
13	Ps. 8	The Son of Man is made a little lower than the angels, and is exalted as ruler over all creation		X	X	X
14	Ps. 40	Messiah volunteers to enter the world, to suffer, and is delivered			X	X
15	Ps. 118	Messiah survives the power of death to become the chief Cornerstone, the Capstone of God's building			X	X

Summary of Messianic Interpretations in the Old Testament, continued

No.	Bible Reference	Summary of the Messianic Prophecy	EJ	NTA	NTE	CF
16	Ps. 78.1-2	Messiah will speak to the people in parables			X	
17	Ps. 69	Messiah's zeal for the house of God will bring hatred and abuse, but his enemies will receive their just dues			X	X
18	Ps. 109	The one who betrays Messiah will suffer a terrible fate			X	X
19	Ps. 22	After unparalleled suffering, Messiah conquers death and rejoices with his brethren			X	X
20	Ps. 2	Messiah is enthroned in Zion, defeats his opposition, and rules over creation	X		X	X
21	Ps. 16	Yahweh will not allow Messiah to see corruption in Sheol			X	X
22	Ps. 102	Messiah the creator is eternal, though suffering severe persecution				X
23	Ps. 45	Messiah is God, and has been anointed by God to sit upon an eternal throne. His people are his lovely bride.	X			X
24	Ps. 110	Messiah is a priest-king after the order of Melchizedek, and he sits at the right hand of God ruling over all humankind	X		X	X
25	Ps. 72	Messiah reigns over a universal and righteous Kingdom of blessing	X			X
26	Ps. 68	Messiah wins a great victory, then ascends back on high	X		X	X
27	Job 9.33; 16.19-21; 17.3; 33.23-28	A Mediator, Interpreter, Advocate, and Witness will walk in the latter days upon the earth				
28	Job 19.23-27	A Redeemer will stand upon the earth in the latter days and the righteous will see him				X
29	Joel 2.23	A Wonderful Teacher will arise and usher in an age of great abundance	X			X
30	Hos. 1.10-2.1	A Second Moses will lead God's people out of bondage into a glorious new era			X	
31	Hos. 3.5	After the exile, God's people will serve Yahweh their God and David their King	X			

Summary of Messianic Interpretations in the Old Testament, continued

No.	Bible Reference	Summary of the Messianic Prophecy	EJ	NTA	NTE	CF
32	Hos. 11.1	God calls his son, the Second Israel, out of Egypt			X	
33	Isa. 4.2-6	The beautiful and glorious Shoot of Yahweh will be the pride of the remnant of Israel	X			
34	Isa. 7.14-15	A virgin will conceive and bear a son whose name will be called Immanuel			X	X
35	Isa. 8.17-18	Messiah waits for the time of his coming, and he and his children are signs and wonders in Israel		X	X	
36	Isa. 9.1-7	Messiah will bring light to Galilee, and one will sit on the throne of David to usher in the reign of God in righteousness and justice	X	X		X
37	Isa. 11.1-16	A Shoot from the stem of Jesse will be filled with the Spirit of Yahweh, and will usher into the earth a Kingdom of righteousness and peace	X	X	X	X
38	Isa. 16.5	Downtrodden peoples will look to the house of David for justice and lovingkindness				
39	Isa. 28.16	God is going to lay in Zion a Tried and Tested Stone, a Precious Cornerstone	X	X	X	X
40	Isa. 30.19-26	The people of God will see their divine Teacher and will enjoy his abundant blessing as a result of listening to him	X			
41	Isa. 32.1-2	A Leader of the future will be a shelter from the storm, like water in a dry place				
42	Isa. 33.17	The eyes of the people of God will see the King in his beauty				
43	Isa. 42.17	Yahweh's Servant will bring forth justice to the nations, and will be a Covenant to the people, a Light to the nations	X		X	X
44	Isa. 49.1-13	Yahweh's Servant is divinely appointed to teach, to raise up the tribes of Jacob, and to be a Light to the Gentiles	X			X
45	Isa. 50.4-11	Yahweh's Servant is an obedient disciple, who endures suffering and indignity				X
46	Isa. 52.13-53.12	God's Servant is rejected, suffers horribly for the sins of others, dies, but then sees his seed and is satisfied	X	X	X	X

Summary of Messianic Interpretations in the Old Testament, continued

No.	Bible Reference	Summary of the Messianic Prophecy	EJ	NTA	NTE	CF
47	Isa. 55.3-5	A son of David will be made a Witness, Leader, and Commander for the peoples				X
48	Isa. 59.20-21	A Redeemer will come to penitent Zion	X		X	
49	Isa. 61.1-11	Messiah has been anointed by the Spirit of Yahweh to proclaim the Good News to the poor, and liberty and deliverance to the captives	X		X	X
50	Mic. 2.12-13	The divine Breaker will lead the people of God out of bondage	X			
51	Mic. 5.1-5	A glorious Ruler will arise from Bethlehem to shepherd the people of God and give them victory over their enemies	X	X	X	X
52	Hab. 3.12-15	Yahweh comes forth from the salvation of his Anointed, and will strike through the head of the house of evil				
53	Jer. 23.5-6	God will raise up a Righteous Branch who will act wisely and execute justice and righteousness in the land	X			
54	Jer. 30.9, 21	Upon return from exile, God's people will serve David their King who will serve as Mediator and draw near to God for them	X			
55	Jer. 31.21-22	God will create a new thing in the land	X			X
56	Jer. 33.14-26	Yahweh will raise up his righteous Servant in the land, and will not fail to fulfill his promise to David and to Levi	X			
57	Ezek. 17.22-24	A tender Twig from the house of David will become a stately Cedar with birds of every kind nesting under it	X			X
58	Ezek. 21.25-27	The crown is removed from the last king of Judah until he comes whose right it is				
59	Ezek. 34.23-31	God will set over those who return from Babylon one Shepherd, his servant David		X		
60	Ezek. 37.21-28	God's people will be united and will have one King, "My Servant David"		X		
61	Ezek. 44.48	A Prince in the future age will be accorded honor, and through him sacrifices will be offered to God	X			

Summary of Messianic Interpretations in the Old Testament, continued

No.	Bible Reference	Summary of the Messianic Prophecy	EJ	NTA	NTE	CF
62	Dan. 7.13-14	One like a Son of Man will come before the Ancient of Days to receive an everlasting Kingdom and dominion	X	X	X	X
63	Dan. 9.24-27	After 69 "weeks" of years, Messiah will appear, he will be cut off, and will cause sacrifice and oblation to cease	X			X
64	Hag. 2-6-9	After the shaking of the nations, the Desire of all Nations will come and fill the Temple of God with glory	X		X	
65	Hag. 2.21-23	Zerubbabel will be made God's signet Ring in the day when the thrones of kingdoms and the Gentiles are overthrown by Yahweh				
66	Zech. 3.8-10	The Servant of Yahweh, his Shoot is symbolized by Joshua the high priest and by an engraved Stone	X			X
67	Zech. 6.12-13	A man whose name is Shoot shall build the Temple of the Lord, and he will be a Priest and a King	X			X
68	Zech. 9.9-11	The King of Zion comes riding upon the foal of a donkey	X		X	X
69	Zech. 10.3-4	God will send one who is the Cornerstone, the tent Peg, the Battle Bow, the One who possesses all sovereignty	X			
70	Zech. 11.4-14	Thirty pieces of silver thrown to the potter in the house of God			X	X
71	Zech. 13.7	The sword of divine justice smites the Shepherd and the sheep are scattered			X	X
72	Mal. 3.1	The LORD's messenger will clear the way before him, and the Lord will suddenly come to his Temple	X	X	X	X
73	Mal. 4.2	The Sun of Righteousness will arise with healing in his wings	X	X		

Appendix 24
Suffering for the Gospel:
The Cost of Discipleship and Servant-Leadership
Rev. Dr. Don L. Davis

To embrace the Gospel and not to be ashamed of it (Rom. 1.16) is to bear the stigma and reproach of the One who called you into service (2 Tim. 3.12). Practically, this may mean the loss of comfort, convenience, and even life itself (John 12.24-25). As ambassadors of Christ, appealing to men and women to come to him, we must not even count our lives as dear to ourselves, but be ever willing to lay our very lives down for the Good News (Acts 20.24). All of Christ's apostles endured insults, rebukes, lashes, and rejections by the enemies of their Master (cf. 2 Cor. 6, 11). Each of them sealed their calling to Christ and to his doctrines with their blood in exile, torture, and martyrdom. Listed below are the fates of the apostles according to traditional accounts.

- *Matthew* suffered martyrdom by being slain with a sword at a distant city of Ethiopia.

- *Mark* expired at Alexandria, after being cruelly dragged through the streets of that city.

- *Luke* was hanged upon an olive tree in the land of Greece.

- *John* was put in a caldron of boiling oil, but escaped death in a miraculous manner, and was afterward exiled to and branded at Patmos.

- *Peter* was crucified at Rome in an inverted position, with his head downward.

- *James, the Greater*, was beheaded at Jerusalem.

- *James, the Less*, was thrown from a lofty pinnacle of the temple, and then beaten to death with a fuller's club.

- *Bartholomew* was flayed alive.

Suffering for the Gospel, continued

- *Andrew* was bound to a cross, where he preached to his persecutors until he died.

- *Thomas* was run through the body with a lance at Coromandel in the East Indies.

- *Jude* was shot to death with arrows.

- *Matthias* was first stoned and then beheaded.

- *Barnabas* of the Gentiles was stoned to death at Salonica.

- *Paul*, after various tortures and persecutions, was at length beheaded at Rome by the Emperor Nero.

And what more shall I say? For time will fail me if I tell of Gideon, Barak, Samson, Jephthah, of David and Samuel and the prophets, who by faith conquered kingdoms, performed acts of righteousness, obtained promises, shut the mouths of lions, quenched the power of fire, escaped the edge of the sword, from weakness were made strong, became mighty in war, put foreign armies to flight. Women received back their dead by resurrection; and others were tortured, not accepting their release, in order that they might obtain a better resurrection; and others experienced mockings and scourgings, yes, also chains and imprisonment. They were stoned, they were sawn in two, they were tempted, they were put to death with the sword; they went about in sheepskins, in goatskins, being destitute, afflicted, ill-treated (men of who the world was not worthy), wandering in deserts and mountains and caves and holes in the ground. And all these, having gained approval through their faith, did not receive what was promised, because God had provided something better for us, so that apart from us they should not be made perfect.

~ Hebrews 11.32-40

Appendix 25
Messiah Yeshua in Every Book of the Bible
Adapted from Norman L. Geisler, *A Popular Survey of the Old Testament*

Christ in the Books of the Old Testament
1. The Seed of the Woman, Gen. 3.15
2. The Passover Lamb, Exod. 12.3-4
3. The Atoning Sacrifice, Lev. 17.11
4. The Smitten Rock, Num. 20.8, 11
5. The Faithful Prophet, Deut. 18.18
6. The Captain of the Lord's Host, Josh. 5.15
7. The Divine Deliverer, Judg. 2.18
8. The Kinsman Redeemer, Ruth 3.12
9. The Anointed One, 1 Sam. 2.10
10. The Son of David, 2 Sam. 7.14
11. The Coming King, 1 Kings
12. The Coming King, 2 Kings
13. The Builder of the Temple, 1 Chron. 28.20
14. The Builder of the Temple, 2 Chron.
15. The Restorer of the Temple, Ezra 6.14, 15
16. The Restorer of the Nation, Neh. 6.15
17. The Preserver of the Nation, Esther 4.14
18. The Living Redeemer, Job 19.25
19. The Praise of Israel, Ps. 150.6
20. The Wisdom of God, Prov. 8.22, 23
21. The Great Teacher, Eccles. 12.11
22. The Fairest of Ten Thousand, Song of Sol. 5.10
23. The Suffering Servant, Isa. 53.11
24. The Maker of the New Covenant, Jer. 31.31
25. The Man of Sorrows, Lam. 3.28-30
26. The Glory of God, Ezek. 43.2
27. The Coming Messiah, Dan. 9.25
28. The Lover of the Unfaithful, Hos. 3.1
29. The Hope of Israel, Joel 3.16
30. The Husbandman, Amos 9.13
31. The Savior, Obad. 21
32. The Resurrected One, Jon. 2.10
33. The Ruler in Israel, Mic. 5.2
34. The Avenger, Nah. 2.1
35. The Holy God, Hab. 1.13
36. The King of Israel, Zeph. 3.15
37. The Desire of Nations, Hag. 2.7
38. The Righteous Branch, Zech. 3.8
39. The Sun of Righteousness, Mal. 4.2

Messiah Yeshua in Every Book of the Bible, continued

Christ in the Books of the New Testament

1. The King of the Jews, Matt. 2.2
2. The Servant of the Lord, Mark 10.45
3. The Son of Man, Luke 19.10
4. The Son of God, John 1.1
5. The Ascended Lord, Acts 1.10
6. The Believer's Righteousness, Rom. 1.17
7. Our Sanctification, 1 Cor. 1.30
8. Our Sufficiency, 2 Cor. 12.9
9. Our Liberty, Gal. 2.4
10. The Exalted Head of the Church, Eph. 1.22
11. The Christian's Joy, Phil. 1.26
12. The Fullness of Deity, Col. 2.9
13. The Believer's Comfort, 1 Thess. 4.16, 17
14. The Believer's Glory, 2 Thess. 1.12
15. The Christian's Preserver, 1 Tim. 4.10
16. The Christian's Rewarder, 2 Tim. 4.8
17. The Blessed Hope, Titus 2.13
18. Our Substitute, Philem. 17
19. The Great High Priest, Heb. 4.15
20. The Giver of Wisdom, James 1.5
21. The Rock, 1 Pet. 2.6
22. The Precious Promise, 2 Pet. 1.4
23. The Life, 1 John
24. The Truth, 2 John
25. The Way, 3 John
26. The Advocate, Jude
27. The King of kings and Lord of lords, Rev. 19.16

Appendix 26
Old Testament Names, Titles, and Epithets for the Messiah
Adapted from Norman L. Geisler, *A Popular Survey of the Old Testament*

1. Advocate, Job 16.19
2. Angel (messenger), Job 33.23
3. Anointed, 1 Sam. 2.19; Ps. 2.2
4. Battle-bow, Zech. 10.4
5. Bethlehem's Ruler, Mic. 5.2
6. Breaker, Mic. 2.13
7. Commander, Isa. 55.4
8. Cornerstone (Capstone), Ps. 118.22; Isa. 28.16
9. Covenant of the People, Isa. 42.6
10. Crusher, Gen. 3.15
11. David, Hos. 3.5; Jer. 30.9
12. Desire of all Nations, Hag. 2.7
13. Eternal One, Ps. 102.25-27
14. Eternal Priest, Ps. 110.4
15. Everlasting Father, Isa. 9.6
16. Faithful Priest, 1 Sam. 2.35
17. Firstborn, Ps. 89.27
18. Forsaken Sufferer, Ps. 22
19. Foundation, Isa. 28.16; Zech. 10.4
20. God, Ps. 45.6-7
21. Head, Hos. 1.11; Mic. 2.13
22. Healer, Isa. 42.7
23. He who Comes, Ps. 118.26
24. Horn of David, Ps. 132.17
25. Immanuel, Isa. 7.14
26. Interpreter, Job 33.23
27. Israel, Hos. 11.1; Isa. 49.3
28. King, Ps. 2.5; Hos. 3.5
29. Lamp for David, Ps. 132.17
30. Last, Job 19.25
31. Launderer, Mal. 3.2
32. Leader, Isa. 55.4
33. Liberator, Isa. 42.7
34. Light, Isa. 9.2
35. Light of the Gentiles, Isa. 42.6; 49.6
36. Lord, Mal. 3.1
37. Man, Zech. 6.12; 13.7
38. Man of Sorrows, Isa. 53.3
39. Mediator, Job 33.23
40. Messenger of the Covenant, Mal. 3.1
41. Messiah-Prince, Dan. 9.25
42. Mighty God, Isa. 9.6
43. Mighty Hero, Ps. 45.3
44. My Equal, Zech. 13.7
45. Nail (peg), Zech. 10.4
46. Our Peace, Mic. 5.5
47. Parable Teller, Ps. 78.1-2
48. Pierced One, Zech. 12.10
49. Poor and Afflicted, Ps. 69.29
50. Priestly Ruler, Jer. 30.21; Zech. 6.13
51. Prince, Ezek. 37.25; 44-48
52. Prince of Peace, Isa. 9.6
53. Proclaimer of Good Tidings to the Poor, Isa. 61.2
54. Prophet like Moses, Deut. 18.15,18
55. Redeemer, Job 19.25; Isa. 59.20
56. Refiner, Mal. 3.2
57. Refuge, Isa. 32.1
58. Rejected Shepherd, Zech. 11
59. Rejected Stone, Ps. 118.22
60. Righteous Shoot, Jer. 23.5; 33.15
61. Root out of Dry Ground, Isa. 53.2
62. Ruler of all Nature, Ps. 8.5-8
63. Ruler of the Earth, Isa. 16.5
64. Scepter, Num. 24.17
65. Second Moses, Hos. 11.1
66. Seed of Abraham, Gen. 12.3; 18.18
67. Seed of David, 2 Sam. 2.12
68. Seed of the Woman, Gen. 3.15
69. Servant, Isa. 42.1; 49.3, 6
70. Shade, Isa. 32.2
71. Shelter, Isa. 32.1
72. Shepherd, Ezek. 34.23; 37.24
73. Shiloh, Gen. 49.10
74. Shoot, Zech. 3.8; 6.12
75. Shoot from the Stump of Jesse, Isa. 11.1
76. Shoot of Yahweh, Isa. 4.2

Old Testament Names, Titles, and Epithets for the Messiah, continued

77. Sign and Wonder, Isa. 8.18
78. Signet Ring, Hag. 2.23
79. Son of God, 2 Sam. 7.14; Ps. 2.7
80. Son of Man, Ps. 8.4; Dan. 7.13
81. Star, Num. 24.17
82. Stone, Zech. 3.9
83. Substitutionary Sufferer, Isa. 53
84. Sun of Righteousness, Mal. 4.5
85. Teacher, Isa. 30.20
86. Teacher for Righteousness, Joel 2.23
87. Tender Shoot, Isa. 53.2
88. Tender Twig, Ezek. 17.22
89. Temple Builder, Zech. 6.12
90. Tent Dweller, Gen. 9.26-27
91. Tested Stone, Isa. 28.16
92. Trailblazer, Ps. 16.11
93. Victor, Ps. 68.18
94. Volunteer, Ps. 40.7
95. Water of Life, Isa. 32.2
96. Witness, Job 16.19
97. Witness to the Peoples, Isa. 55.4
98. Wonderful Counselor, Isa. 9.6
99. Yahweh, Our Righteousness, Jer. 23.6
100. Zerubbabel, Hag. 2.23

Appendix 27
Messiah Jesus: Fulfillment of the Old Testament Types
Adapted from Norman L. Geisler, *To Understand the Bible, Look for Jesus*, pp. 38-41

Messiah Jesus Fulfills the Tabernacle Types	
Tabernacle Types	**Jesus of Nazareth as the Antitype**
The One Door	I am the Door John 10.9
The Brazen Altar	Gives his life as a ransom for many Mark 10.45
The Laver	If I do not wash you, you have no part with me John 13.8, 10; 1 John 1.7
The Lampstand	I am the Light of the World John 8.12
The Shewbread	I am the Bread of Life John 6.48
The Altar of Incense	I am praying for them John 17.9
The Veil	This is my body Matt. 26.26
The Mercy Seat	I lay down my life for the sheep John 10.15

Messiah Jesus: Fulfillment of the Old Testament Types, continued

Contrast between Aaron's and Melchizedek's Priesthood		
Nature of the Order	**The Order of Aaron's Levitical Priesthood**	**The Order of Messiah Jesus' Priesthood (Melchizedek's Priesthood)**
Consecration	Temporal and fading	Eternal priesthood Heb. 7.21-23
Priest	Fallible, vulnerable to sin	Sinless and perfect Heb. 7.26
Priesthood	Changeable	Unchangeable priesthood Heb. 7.24
Ministry	Continual offering of sacrifice	Secured an eternal redemption once for all Heb. 9.12, 26
Mediation	Imperfect representation	Perfect representation between God and humankind Heb. 2.14-18
Sacrifice	Unable and insufficient to take the sin of the offenders away	Offered a single sacrifice for sin for all time Heb. 10.11-12
Intercession	Was interrupted by weakness and death	Always lives to make intercession for us Heb. 7.25

Messiah Jesus: Fulfillment of the Old Testament Types, continued

Messiah Jesus Fulfills the Levitical Sacrifices and Offerings	
The Levitical Offering	**How Offering Is Fulfilled in Jesus of Nazareth**
The Burnt Offering	The perfection of his life Heb. 9.14
The Meal Offering	The dedication and presentation of his life Heb. 5.7; John 4.34
The Peace Offering	He is the peace of our relationships and souls Heb. 4.1f.; Eph. 2.14
The Sin Offering	He bore the penalty for our offense Heb. 10.12; 1 John 2.2
The Trespass Offering	Provision for the offender Heb. 10.20f.; 1 John 1.7

Messiah Jesus: Fulfillment of the Old Testament Types, continued

Messiah Jesus Fulfills the Levitical Feasts and Festivals	
Levitical Feast (Lev. 23)	**The Fulfillment in Jesus of Nazareth**
The Passover (April)	The death of Jesus Christ 2 Cor. 5.17
Unleavened Bread (April)	Holy and humble walk for Jesus 1 Cor. 5.8
First Fruits (April)	The resurrection of Messiah Jesus 1 Cor. 15.23
The Feast of Pentecost (June)	Outpouring of the Spirit by the Father and the Son Acts 1.5; 2.4
Trumpets (September)	Messiah Jesus' regathering of the Nation Israel Matt. 24.31
The Day of Atonement (September)	Propitiation and cleansing through Jesus Rom. 11.26
Tabernacles (September)	Rest and reunion with Messiah Jesus Zech. 14.16-18

Appendix 28
The Shadow and the Substance: Understanding the Old Testament as God's Witness to Jesus Christ
Rev. Dr. Don L. Davis

The Law
(Genesis - Deuteronomy)
Foundation for Christ

History
(Joshua - Esther)
Preparation for Christ

Poetry
(Job - Song of Solomon)
Aspiration for Christ

Prophecy
(Isaiah - Malachi)
Expectation of Christ

- Song, Aspiration, and Longing in Worship and Devotion
- The Righteous Demands of the Old Testament Moral Law
- The Patriarchs and the Covenants
- Appearances of the Angel of the Lord (Theophanies)
- Types and Foreshadowings in People, Places, Things, and Events
- The Tabernacle
- The Temple Sacrifices and Festivals
- Prophecies Concerning the Kingdom of God
- Offices of the Prophets, Priesthood, and King
- Old Testament Messianic Prophecy
- Gentile Inclusion in the Salvation of God
- Adam and the History of Israel as Recapitulation

Appendix 29
Analytical vs. Christocentric Approach to Old Testament Study
Rev. Dr. Don L. Davis

Comparing an Analytical Approach with a Christo-centric Approach to the Old Testament	
An Analytical Approach	**A Christo-centric Approach**
Focuses on individual verses, chapters, books, and sections in and of themselves	Focuses on how the content of book points to and gives witness to Messiah Jesus
Breaks Old Testament into many pieces for analysis and exegesis	Looks at Old Testament as single whole which gives single witness to Jesus
Concentrates on studying each book as its own self-contained unit	Concentrates on studying each book as it provides contribution to Christ's coming
Demands linguistic and socio-cultural expertise	Demands spiritual wisdom and discernment
Can only be legitimately done by experts	Can be done by all the saints of God
Difficult to give overview of Old Testament	Uses Christ as key to the interpretation of the Old Testament overview
Focuses on knowledge of content	Focuses on developing relationship to Christ
Hard to disciple others in knowledge of Old Testament and its contents	Designed to help teachers ground believers in the knowledge of Christ through the Old Testament
Can be remarkably boring and dry	Stirs the heart in longing and love for Jesus

Appendix 30
From Deep Ignorance to Credible Witness: Stages of Dynamic Growth
Rev. Dr. Don L. Davis

Witness - Ability to give witness and teach — 8
2 Tim. 2.2
Matt. 28.18-20
1 John 1.1-4
Prov. 20.6
2 Cor. 5.18-21

> *And the things you have heard me say in the presence of many witnesses entrust to reliable men who will also be qualified to teach others.*
> ~ 2 Tim. 2.2

Lifestyle - Consistent appropriation and habitual practice based on beliefs — 7
Heb. 5.11-6.2
Eph. 4.11-16
2 Pet. 3.18
1 Tim. 4.7-10

> *And Jesus increased in wisdom and in stature, and in favor with God and man.*
> ~ Luke 2.52

Demonstration - Expressing conviction in corresponding conduct, speech, and behavior — 6
James 2.14-26
2 Cor. 4.13
2 Pet. 1.5-9
1 Thess. 1.3-10

> *Nevertheless, at your word I will let down the net.*
> ~ Luke 5.5

Conviction - Committing oneself to think, speak, and act in light of information — 5
Heb. 2.3-4
Heb. 11.1, 6
Heb. 3.15-19
Heb. 4.2-6

> *Do you believe this?*
> ~ John 11.26

Discernment - Understanding the meaning and implications of information — 4
John 16.13
Eph. 1.15-18
Col. 1.9-10
Isa. 6.10; 29.10

> *Do you understand what you are reading?*
> ~ Acts 8.30

Knowledge - Ability to recall and recite information — 3
2 Tim. 3.16-17
1 Cor. 2.9-16
1 John 2.20-27
John 14.26

> *For what does the Scripture say?*
> ~ Rom. 4.3

Interest - Responding to ideas or information with both curiosity and openness — 2
Ps. 42.1-2
Acts 9.4-5
John 12.21
1 Sam. 3.4-10

> *We will hear you again on this matter.*
> ~ Acts 17.32

Awareness - General exposure to ideas and information — 1
Mark 7.6-8
Acts 19.1-7
John 5.39-40
Matt. 7.21-23

> *At that time, Herod the tetrarch heard about the fame of Jesus.*
> ~ Matt. 14.1

Ignorance - Unfamiliarity with information due to naivete, indifference, or hardness — 0
Eph. 4.17-19
Ps. 2.1-3
Rom. 1.21; 2.19
1 John 2.11

> *Who is the Lord that I should heed his voice?*
> ~ Exod. 5.2

Appendix 31
In Christ
Rev. Dr. Don L. Davis

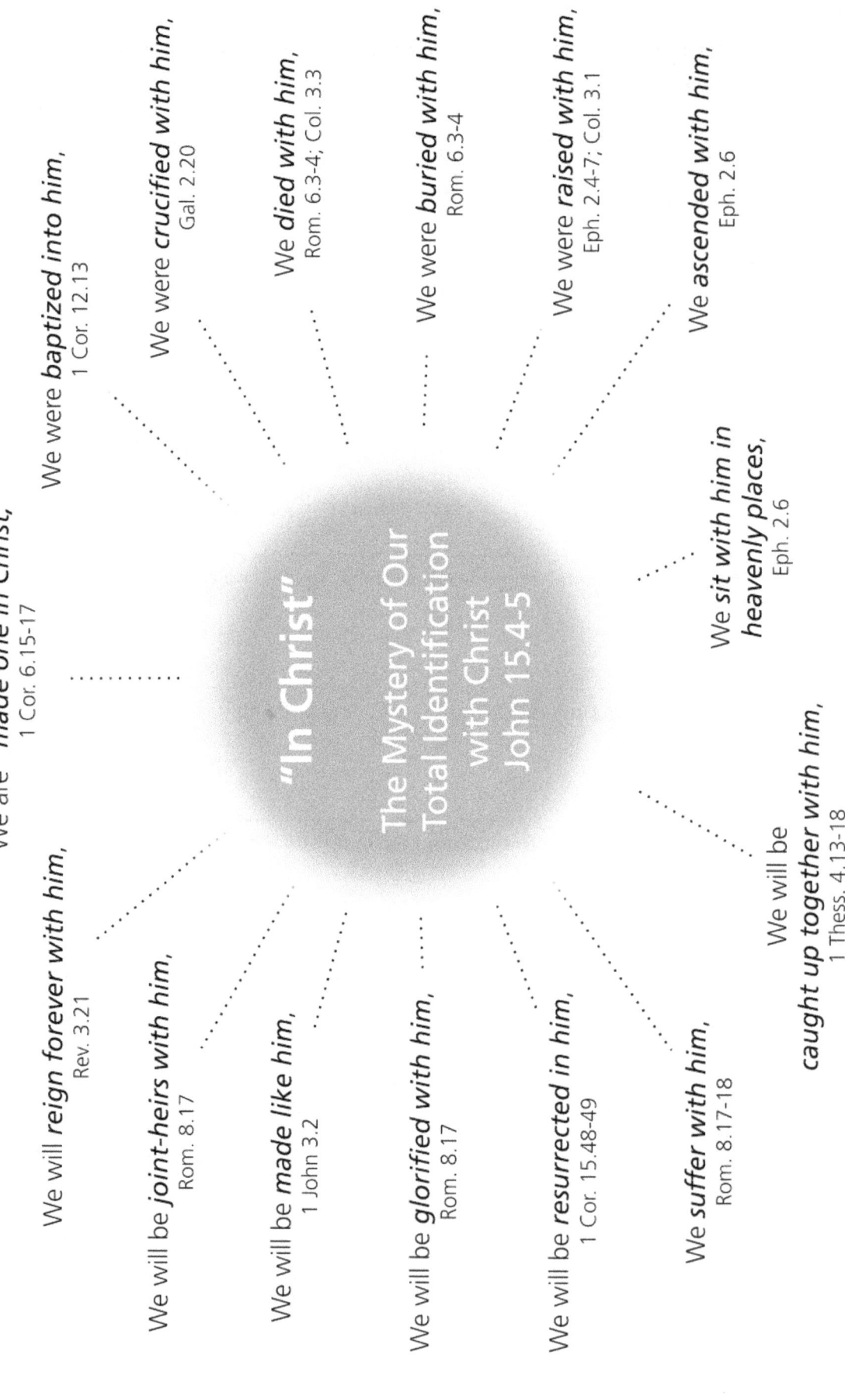

Appendix 32
Substitute Centers to a Christ-Centered Vision
Goods and Effects Which Our Culture Substitutes as the Ultimate Concern
Rev. Dr. Don L. Davis

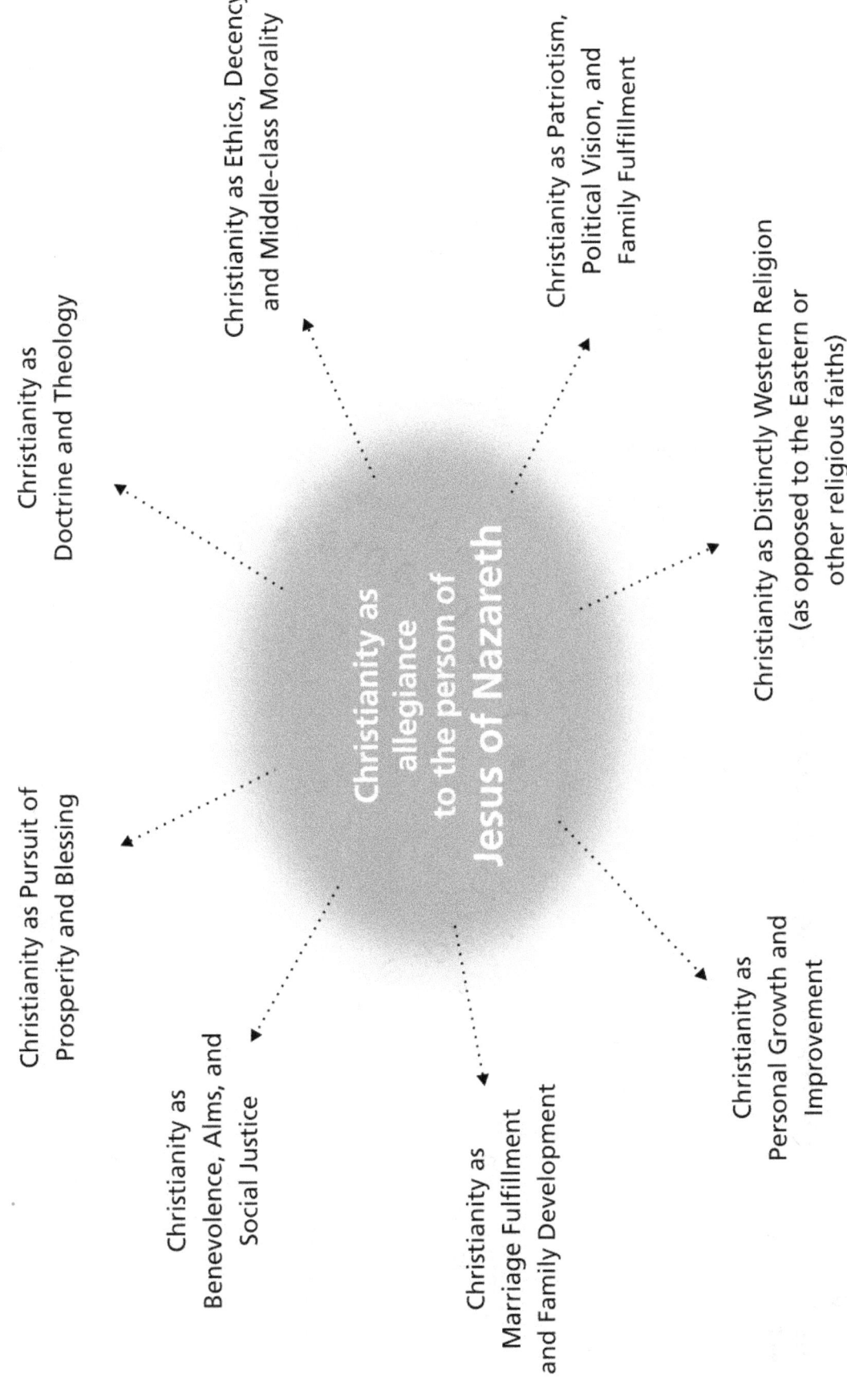

Appendix 33
The Picture and the Drama: Image and Story in the Recovery of Biblical Myth
Rev. Dr. Don L. Davis

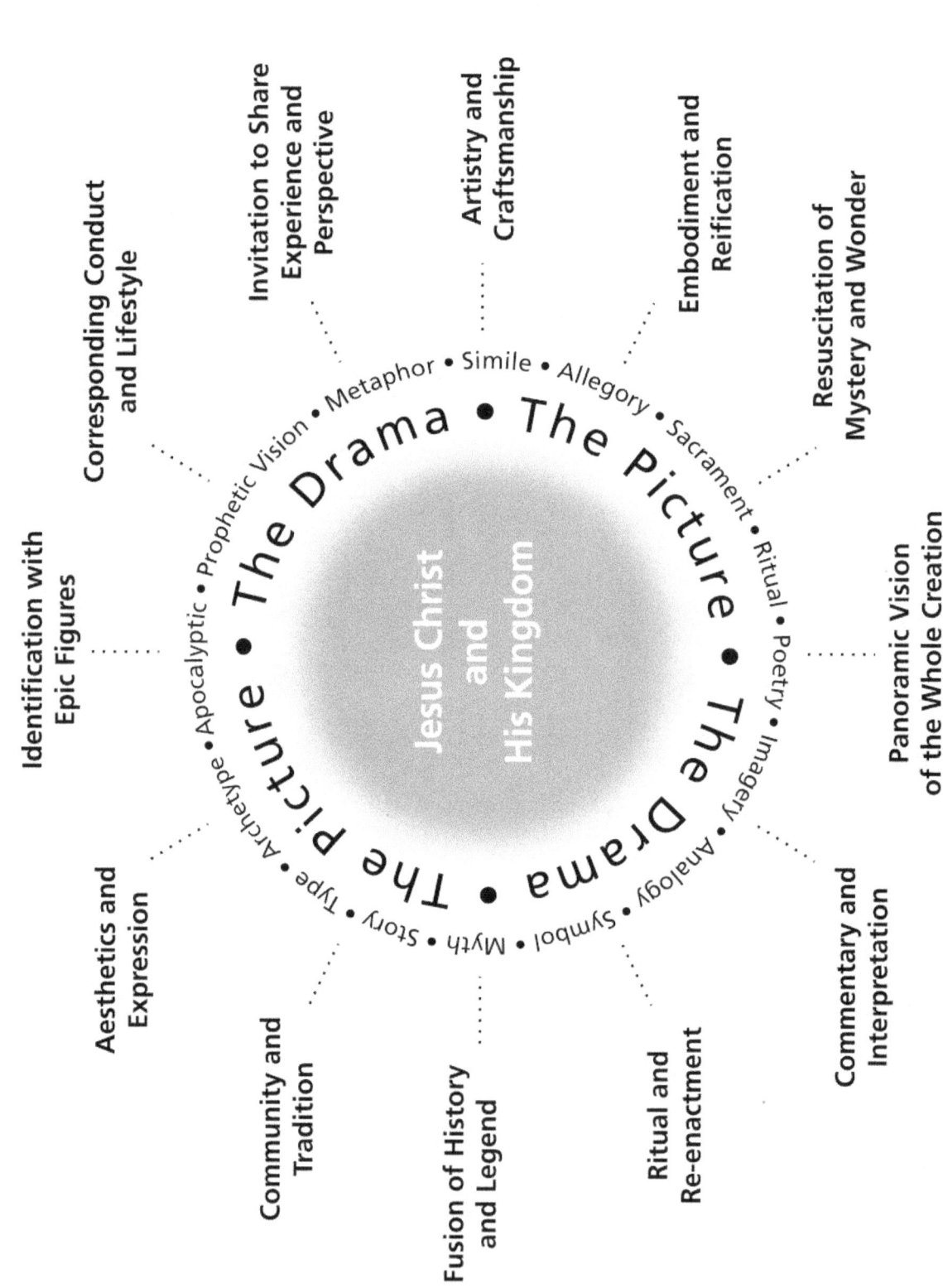

Appendix 34
Union with Christ: The Christocentric Paradigm
Christianity as Union with, Allegiance to, and Devotion to Jesus of Nazareth
Representative texts compiled by Rev. Dr. Don L. Davis

Rom. 6.4-5 (ESV) - We were buried therefore with him by baptism into death, in order that, just as Christ was raised from the dead by the glory of the Father, we too might walk in newness of life. [5] For if we have been united with him in a death like his, we shall certainly be united with him in a resurrection like his.

Col. 2.6-7 (ESV) - Therefore, as you received Christ Jesus the Lord, so walk in him, [7] rooted and built up in him and established in the faith, just as you were taught, abounding in thanksgiving.

John 14.6 (ESV) - Jesus said to him, "I am the way, and the truth, and the life. No one comes to the Father except through me."

Gal. 2.20 (ESV) - It is no longer I who live, but Christ who lives in me. And the life I now live in the flesh I live by faith in the Son of God, who loved me and gave himself for me.

Eph. 2.4-7 (ESV) - But God, being rich in mercy, because of the great love with which he loved us, [5] even when we were dead in our trespasses, made us alive together with Christ - by grace you have been saved - [6] and raised us up with him and seated us with him in the heavenly places in Christ Jesus, [7] so that in the coming ages he might show the immeasurable riches of his grace in kindness toward us in Christ Jesus.

Rom. 8.16-17 (ESV) - The Spirit himself bears witness with our spirit that we are children of God, [17] and if children, then heirs - heirs of God and fellow heirs with Christ, provided we suffer with him in order that we may also be glorified with him.

Eph. 5.2 (ESV) - And walk in love, as Christ loved us and gave himself up for us, a fragrant offering and sacrifice to God.

John 15.4-5 (ESV) - Abide in me, and I in you. As the branch cannot bear fruit by itself, unless it abides in the vine, neither can you,

Union with Christ: The Christocentric Paradigm, continued

unless you abide in me. [5] I am the vine; you are the branches. Whoever abides in me and I in him, he it is that bears much fruit, for apart from me you can do nothing.

Col. 3.17 (ESV) - And whatever you do, in word or deed, do everything in the name of the Lord Jesus, giving thanks to God the Father through him.

1 John 2.6 (ESV) - whoever says he abides in him ought to walk in the same way in which he walked.

Gal. 5.24 (ESV) - And those who belong to Christ Jesus have crucified the flesh with its passions and desires.

Rom. 8.29 (ESV) - For those whom he foreknew he also predestined to be conformed to the image of his Son, in order that he might be the firstborn among many brothers.

Rom. 13.14 (ESV) - But put on the Lord Jesus Christ, and make no provision for the flesh, to gratify its desires.

1 Cor. 15.49 (ESV) - Just as we have borne the image of the man of dust, we shall also bear the image of the man of heaven.

2 Cor. 3.18 (ESV) - And we all, with unveiled face, beholding the glory of the Lord, are being transformed into the same image from one degree of glory to another. For this comes from the Lord who is the Spirit.

Phil. 3.7-8 (ESV) - But whatever gain I had, I counted as loss for the sake of Christ. [8] Indeed, I count everything as loss because of the surpassing worth of knowing Christ Jesus my Lord. For his sake I have suffered the loss of all things and count them as rubbish, in order that I may gain Christ.

Phil. 3.20-21 (ESV) - But our citizenship is in heaven, and from it we await a Savior, the Lord Jesus Christ, [21] who will transform our lowly body to be like his glorious body, by the power that enables him even to subject all things to himself.

Union with Christ: The Christocentric Paradigm, continued

1 John 3.2 (ESV) - Beloved, we are God's children now, and what we will be has not yet appeared; but we know that when he appears we shall be like him, because we shall see him as he is.

John 17.16 (ESV) - They are not of the world, just as I am not of the world.

Col. 1.15-18 (ESV) - He is the image of the invisible God, the firstborn of all creation. [16] For by him all things were created, in heaven and on earth, visible and invisible, whether thrones or dominions or rulers or authorities - all things were created through him and for him. [17] And he is before all things, and in him all things hold together. [18] And he is the head of the body, the church. He is the beginning, the firstborn from the dead, that in everything he might be preeminent.

Heb. 2.14-15 (ESV) - Since therefore the children share in flesh and blood, he himself likewise partook of the same things, that through death he might destroy the one who has the power of death, that is, the devil, [15] and deliver all those who through fear of death were subject to lifelong slavery.

Rev. 1.5-6 (ESV) - and from Jesus Christ the faithful witness, the firstborn of the dead, and the ruler of kings on earth. To him who loves us and has freed us from our sins by his blood [6] and made us a kingdom, priests to his God and Father, to him be glory and dominion forever and ever. Amen.

2 Tim. 2.11-13 (ESV) - The saying is trustworthy, for: If we have died with him, we will also live with him; [12] if we endure, we will also reign with him; if we deny him, he also will deny us; [13] if we are faithless, he remains faithful—for he cannot deny himself.

Rev. 3.21 (ESV) - The one who conquers, I will grant him to sit with me on my throne, as I also conquered and sat down with my Father on his throne.

Appendix 35
Typology
Evangelical Dictionary of Theology, Walter A. Elwell (ed.)
Baker Books: Grand Rapids, Michigan. 1984. pp. 1117-1119

From the Greek word for form or pattern, which in biblical times denoted both the original model or prototype and the copy that resulted. In the NT the latter was labeled the antitype, and this was especially used in two directions: (1) the correspondence between two historical situations like the flood and baptism (I Pet. 3:21) or two figures like Adam and Christ (Rom. 5:14); (2) the correspondence between the heavenly pattern and its earthly counterpart, e.g., the divine original behind the earthly tent/tabernacle (Acts 7:44; Heb. 8:5; 9:24). There are several categories – persons (Adam, Melchizedek), events (flood, brazen serpent), institutions (feast), places (Jerusalem, Zion), objects (altar of burnt offering, incense), offices (prophet, priest, king).

In addition we might note the parallel use of image along with type to denote a moral example to be followed. This latter is an important part of the NT stress on imitation of the divinely ordained pattern exemplified first in Christ (John 13:15; I Pet. 2:21), then in the apostolic band (Phil. 3:17; II Thess. 3:9), the leaders (I Tim. 4:12; Titus 2:7; I Pet. 5:3), and the community itself (I Thess. 1:7). As such all believers are to consider themselves models or patterns of the Christlike life.

It is important to distinguish types from symbol and allegory. A symbol has a meaning apart from its normal semantic field and goes beyond it to stand for an abstract concept, e.g., cross = life, fire = judgment. Allegory is a series of metaphors in which each one adds an element to form a composite picture of the message, e.g., in the good shepherd allegory (John 10) each part carries meaning. Typology, however, deals with the principle of analogous fulfillment. A symbol is an abstract correspondence, while a type is an actual historical event or person. An allegory compares two distinct entities and involves a story or extended development of figurative expressions while a type is a specific parallel between two historical entities; the former is indirect and implicit, the latter direct and explicit. Therefore, biblical typology involves an analogical correspondence in which earlier events, persons, and places in salvation history become patterns by which later events and the like are interpreted.

Typology, continued

Hermeneutical Significance. It has increasingly been recognized that typology expresses the basic hermeneutic, indeed the attitude or perspective, by which both OT and NT writers understood themselves and their predecessors. Each new community in the ongoing development of salvation history viewed itself analogously in terms of the past. This is true within the OT as well as in the NT use of the OT. The two major sources, of course, were creation and the Exodus. Creation typology is especially seen in Rom. 5 and the Adm-Christ parallel, while Exodus or covenant typology predominates in both testaments. Positively, the Exodus was behind the redemptive imagery in Isa. 51-52 as well as NT salvific concepts (e.g., I Cor. 10:1-6). Negatively, the wilderness wanderings became the model for future admonition (e.g., Ps. 95:7-8; Heb. 4:3-11).

The church fathers combined typology and allegory, linking the former with general religious truths expressed in terms of Greek philosophical concepts. This continued until the Reformation (with periodic opposition such as the Antiochene school of the fourth century or the Victorenes of the twelfth); the Reformers espoused a system which viewed the OT literally with a Christological hermeneutic, i.e., as pointing forward messianically to Christ. During the critical period after the seventeenth century, the whole concept of promise-fulfillment was played down and the OT became religious experience rather than history. In recent decades, however, typology properly conceived has become again a valid tool, based upon the biblical perspective regarding the recurring pattern in God's acts within history, thereby establishing continuity between the stages of redemptive history.

Current Debate. The debate today concerns the possible distinction between innate and inferred types. An innate type is explicitly stated as such in the NT; an inferred type is not explicitly but is established by the general tone of NT teaching, e.g., the Epistle to the Hebrews, which uses typology as its basic hermeneutic. Many deny the latter because of the danger of fanciful eisegesis which subjectively twists the text.

Both type and antitype should be based upon genuine historical parallels rather than timeless mythological parallels. Typology should not redefine the meaning of the text or suggest superficial rather than genuine correspondence. Both OT and NT passages should be exegeted before parallels are drawn.

Typology, continued

Further, one should study the specific correspondences as well as the differences between type and antitype. Here typology is similar to parable research, necessitating a consideration of exegetical details in both OT and NT passages. In what way, e.g., was the brazen serpent a type of Jesus' death in John 3:14-15? Were the peripheral details of Num. 21:4-9 part of the typology? There will always be a single central point, and secondary details must be noted with care before they are applied to the analogy. Noting the dissimilarities provides a control against an overly imaginative, allegorical rendering of the type.

It is well to avoid dogmatizing types. It is difficult and extremely subjective to establish doctrine on the basis of typology. Even in Heb., typology is utilized for illustrative effect rather than for dogmatic considerations. Therefore, only when typology has a direct doctrinal purpose may we affirm such.

> Finally, one must not seek types where the context does not warrant them. As in all exegetical study, we want to arrive at the author's intended meaning rather than a generalized subjective interpretation. As stated above, while the NT writers undoubtedly used typology that is not recorded in canon, we do not have the revelatory stance necessary to extend that approach beyond the text itself. The allegorical, subjective results seen in many modern sermons testify eloquently to the dangers.
>
> - G.R. Osborne

Bibliography

E. Achtemeier. *IDB* Supplement, 926-27; D.L. Baker, "Typology and the Christian Use of the OT," *SJT* 29:137-57; E.C. Blackman, "Return to Typology," *CongQ* 32:53-59; J.W. Drane, "Typology," *EvQ* 50:195-210; E.E. Ellis, "How the NT Uses the Old," in *NT Interpretation*, ed. I H. Marshall; A.M. Fairbairn, *The Typology of Scripture*; F. Foulkes, *The Acts of God: A Study of the Basis of Typology in the OT*; L. Goppelt, *Typos: The Typological Interpretation of the NT* and *TDNT*, VIII, 246-59; S. Gundry, "Typology as a Means of Interpretation," *JETS* 12:233-40; H. Hammel, "The OT Basis of Typological Interpretation," *BR* 9:38-50; G.H. Lampe and K.J. Woolcombe, *Essays on Typology*; R.B. Laurin, "Typological Interpretation of the OT," in *Baker's Dictionary of Practical Theology*, ed. R. Turnbull; H. Muller, *NIDNTT*, III 903-7; N. H. Ridderbos, "Typology," *VoxT* 31:149-50; J. Stek, "Biblical Typology: Yesterday and Today," *CTJ* 5:133-62.

Appendix 36
Typology Readings
Rev. Dr. Don L. Davis

The Study of Types Critical to New Testament Mastery

There are many passages in the New Testament which we cannot understand without having become in some measure familiar with the types. The epistle to the Hebrews is almost entirely made up of references to the Old Testament: as the substance, Christ, is proved to be better than the shadows–better than Moses, than Joshua, than Abraham, than Aaron, than the first Tabernacle, than the Levitical sacrifices, than the whole cloud of witnesses in the picture gallery of faith; and lastly, his blood is proved to be better than the blood of Abel.

We sometimes forget that the writers of the New Testament were *students of the Old Testament*; that it was *their Bible*, and that they would naturally allude again and again to the types and shadows, expecting their readers also to be familiar with them. *If we fail to see these allusions, we lose much of the beauty of the passage, and cannot rightly understand it.* . . .

[The study of types] gives us a sure antidote for the poison of the so-called "higher criticism." If we acknowledge the Divine intention of every detail of the types, even though we may not understand all their teaching, and if we believe there is a lesson in every incident recorded, the attacks of modern criticism will not harm us. We may not be clear enough to understand what the critics say, or to answer their criticisms; but *if our eyes have been opened to see the beauty of the types, the doubts which such writers suggest will not trouble us, and we shall have a more profitable occupation than reading their works*. When so much of this destructive criticism is about, we cannot do better than urge all–even the youngest Christians–to take up the typical study of God's Word; for though *he has hid these things from the wise and prudent, he reveals them unto babes*.

~ Ada R. Habershon, *Study of the Types*.
Grand Rapids: Kregel Publishing, (1957) 1974. pp. 19, 21

Do We Presently Study the Bible in the Same Way and with the Same Methods as the Lord and the Apostles?

After more than twenty years of teaching the grammatical-historical hermeneutic, I can see only one problem with it: it doesn't appear to be the way the biblical writers always did it! When we examine how the biblical writers used previously written Scripture, we see that

Typology Readings, continued

they seemed to "discover" meaning there that, judged by its original context, can hardly be imagined to have been in the mind of the original author. This problem is especially evident in the way the New Testament authors used Old Testament passages to prove that Jesus Christ fulfilled prophecy (or to make some theological point.)

~ James DeYoung and Sarah Hurty, *Beyond the Obvious*. Gresham, OR: Vision House Publishing, 1995. p. 24

Can or Should We Reproduce the Exegesis of the New Testament?

To the question whether we can reproduce the exegesis of the New Testament, S. L. Johnson answers: "Unhesitatingly the reply is yes, although we are not allowed to claim for our results the infallibility of the Lord and his Apostles. They are reliable teachers of biblical doctrine and they are reliable teachers of hermeneutics and exegesis. We not only can reproduce their exegetical methodology, we must if we are to be taught their understanding of the Scriptures."

~ James DeYoung and Sarah Hurty, *Beyond the Obvious*. p. 265

What of Typology as a Valid, Important Method of Bible Interpretation?

[Typology] is a genuine approach widely practiced in the New Testament. For example, the furniture of the tabernacle and other matters associated with it and the temple (the altar and sacrifices, the veil, the golden cover of the ark of the covenant) are all types of Christ and of the heavenly realm (see Heb. 9). When we come to typology, we must avoid being too broad or too narrow in our interpretation. We can be too broad if we find typology everywhere. We can be too narrow if we reject typology as an exegetical method on the basis of the claim that it is not consistent with a literal meaning which embraces on meaning, found by means of grammatical-historical study. . . .

Yet we believe that typology is not to be divorced from exegesis, even though it cannot be fully "regulated hermeneutically, but takes place in the freedom of the Holy Spirit." It very much involves a deeper meaning and was readily practiced by the Bible in its exegetical method (see 1 Cor. 10; Rom. 5).

~ James DeYoung and Sarah Hurty, *Beyond the Obvious*. p. 74

Diverse Usages of the Term Typos in the New Testament

The language of Scripture being essentially popular, its use of particular terms naturally partakes of the freedom and variety which

Typology Readings, continued

are wont to appear in the current speech of a people; and it rarely if ever happens that words are employed, in respect to topics requiring theological treatment, with such precision and uniformity as to enable us, from this source alone, to attain to proper accuracy and fullness.

The word type (***typos***) forms no exception to this usage.

Occurring once, at least, in the natural sense of *mark* or *impress* made by a hard substance on one of softer material (John 20.25)

It commonly bears the general import of *model*, *pattern*, or *exemplar*, but with such a wide diversity of application as to comprehend a material object of worship, or idol (Acts 7.43)

An *external framework* constructed for the service of God (Acts 7.44; Heb. 8.5)

The *form* or *copy* of an epistle (Acts 23.25)

A *method of doctrinal instruction* delivered by the first heralds and teachers of the Gospel (Rom. 7.17)

A *representative character*, or, in certain respects, normal example (Rom. 5.14; 1 Cor. 10.11; Phil. 3.17; 1 Thess. 1.7; 1 Pet. 5.3)

Such in the New Testament Scriptures is the diversified use of the word *type* (disguised, however, under other terms in the authorized version).

~ Patrick Fairbairn, *Typology of Scripture*.
Grand Rapids: Kregel Publishing. p. 42

Extreme Misuse of Typology Is Very Possible

We marvel with peculiar awe at the ability and agility which some well-meaning brethren display in seeing what is not there; as also we marvel, with a sense of our denseness, at the super-spirituality which they evince in aerifying the most unsuspicious details of Scripture into rare spiritual significances.

The "three white baskets" which Pharaoh's ill-fated baker dreamed were on his head are to ourselves part of a true story; but to see in those same three basket recondite bearings upon the doctrine of the Trinity makes one part of our mind laugh and another part groan. We feel the same sort of reaction when we are assured that the bride's

Typology Readings, continued

hair in the Song of Solomon is the mass of the nations converted to Christianity.

It is an eye-opener to learn that the "two pence" which the Good Samaritan gave to the innkeeper were covertly Baptism and the Lord's Supper. We cannot but feel sorry for Matthew, Mark, Luke and John, when another ministerial victim of typomania tells us the "four barrels" of water which Elijah commanded to be poured over the altar on Mount Carmel were the four Gospel writers.

As for the clergyman who would persuade us the boat in which our Lord crossed Galilee is the Church of England, while the "other little ships" which accompanied it were the other denominations, we cannot shake off a sly idea that the novel expositor himself, like the boats, must have been all "at sea." We feel just the same about Pope Gregory the Great's exposition of Job, in which Job's verbose "friends" typify heretics; and his sevens sons the twelve Apostles; his seven thousand sheep God's faithful people and his three thousand hump-backed camels the depraved Gentiles!"

~ J. Sidlow Baxter, *The Strategic Grasp of the Bible*.

The Three Errors of Typology to Avoid

There are three dangers, however, which must be avoided:
Limiting the type, and therefore not using it
Exaggerating the type, and therefore overusing it
Imagining the type, and therefore misusing it

~ J. Boyd Nicholson from the foreword to *Harvest Festivals*.

The Case Against the "Older View" of Typology

The case against typology:

Concerned only with finding "prefigurations" of Christ all over the Old Testament

God ordained Old Testament events, institutions, and/or persons for the primary purpose of foreshadowing Christ.

Two bad results of this old hermeneutic:

Typology Readings, continued

No need to find much reality and meaning in the events and persons themselves (Old Testament) becomes nothing more than a collection of shadows)

Interpreted every obscure detail of Old Testament "type" as a foreshadowing of Jesus (hermeneutics becomes magic, like pulling a rabbit out of a hat)

Conclusion: typology is not the way of interpreting the Old Testament for itself. "But when we go back and read the whole of Psalm 2, Isaiah 42 and Genesis 22, it is equally true that they have enormous depths of truth and meaning for us to explore which are not directly related to Jesus himself. Typology is a way of helping us understand Jesus in the light of the Old Testament. It is not the exclusive way to understand the full meaning of the Old Testament itself" (Wright, 116).

~ Christopher J. H. Wright, *Knowing Jesus through the Old Testament*. Downers Grove: InterVarsity Press, 1992. pp. 115-116

Rebutting Wright's Claims:

Jesus used typology (e.g., the brazen serpent, manna in the wilderness, the Temple of his body, the Good Shepherd, etc.)

The Apostles and early Christian interpreters used typology as their normal way of reading the Old Testament (e.g., Moses' striking the Rock, the wilderness journey of the nation of Israel, Jesus as the second Israel, etc.)

The Bible refers to itself in this way (e.g., the Book of Hebrews, the Tabernacle, the priesthood, etc.)

The question: Should we use the Old Testament as Jesus and the Apostles did, with some reference to *typology*?

The Christological Hermeneutic: Messiah Jesus Connects the Testaments

Christ at once sums up in himself the *perfection of the Old Testament precepts, the substance of Old Testament shadows and types, and the fulfillment of Old Testament forecasts*. Those truths about him which bud forth in the Old Testament come into full bloom in the New Testament; the flashlight of prophetic truth turns into the floodlight of divine revelation.

Typology Readings, continued

The Old Testament foreshadows find their fulfillment in the New Testament in several ways: (1) The *moral precepts* of the Old Testament become fulfilled or perfected in the life and teachings of Christ. (2) The *ceremonial* and *typical* truths were only shadows of the true substance to be found in Christ. (3) The *Messianic prophecies* foretold in the Old Testament were finally fulfilled in the history of the New Testament. In each of these relationships it can be seen that the Testaments are inseparably connected. The New is not only supplementary to the Old but it is the necessary complement to it.

As the book of Hebrews puts it, "God had foreseen something better for us, that apart from us they [Old Testament believers] should not be made perfect" (Heb. 11.40). For what was contained in the Old Testament is fully explained only in the New Testament.

~ Norman Geisler, *To Understand the Bible Look for Jesus.* (1979) 2002. p. 68

The Way Paul and the Apostles Read Scripture

As can be clearly seen, the hermeneutical procedure which Paul and the other New Testament authors use to interpret the Law in a spiritual sense is allegorical, in that a meaning other than the literal or immediate sense is perceived from the given text. The usual term which Paul employs to define the relationship between the two levels of meaning is *typos* = form, figure, symbol, or prefiguration (Rom. 5.14; 1 Cor. 10.6, etc.); but in Galatians 4.24, where he presents the sons of Hagar and Sarah as prefigurations of the Jews and Christians, he says 'Now this is an allegory (*allegoroumena*), showing that he regarded 'typos' as synonymous with 'allegory.'

In deference to Paul's terminology, modern scholars call this kind of interpretation - which, as we shall see, enjoyed immense success and became the authentic Christian way of reading the Old Testament - 'typology' or 'typological interpretation.' In antiquity [i.e., in olden times] it was called 'spiritual' or 'mystical.'

It was rooted in the firm conviction that the old Law was consistently directed towards the great Christ-event, and that, as a result, it would give up its true significance only to those who interpreted it in Christological terms.

~ Manlo Simonetti, *Biblical Interpretation in the Early Church.* p. 11-12

Appendix 37
With Him
Richard Baxter

Lord, it belongs not to my care
Whether I die or live:
To love and serve *Thee* is my share,
And this *Thy* grace must give.

Christ leads me through no darker rooms
Than *He* went through before;
He that unto God's kingdom comes
Must enter by *this* door.

My knowledge of that life is small,
The eye of faith is dim;
But 'tis enough that Christ knows all,
And I shall be *with Him*.

Appendix 38
Focus on Christ
John W. Stott

The greatest need is to see Christ in every situation and every relationship.

We must not put him in a corner or lock him up in a cupboard.

We must not attempt to restrict him to Sundays or churches or Bibles or the religious bit of our lives.

On the contrary, we must *welcome him* into, indeed *discover him* in, every part and every moment of our lives. *We need therefore to pray that the Holy Spirit will make Christ real to us*, since it is his distinctive ministry to do so, namely to 'glorify' or manifest Christ.

Also we must be *disciplined in seeking our Lord's face every day and bringing our life and work to him in prayer,* for then gradually his presence will pervade the whole of our life, and it will become natural for us to turn to him and talk to him at any time.

Then too we shall *see him in or behind others*, and seeing him shall treat them as we would treat him. This is what it means to live "unto Christ."

~ John W. Stott. *Focus on Christ.*
Cleveland: William Collins, 1979. p. 118.

Appendix 39
Theological Support for the Position That Jesus Could Have Sinned Had He Chosen to Do So
Rev. Dr. Don L. Davis

The sinlessness of our Lord does not amount to absolute impeccability. As a true man He must have been capable of sinning. That He did not sin under the greatest provocation, that when He was reviled He blessed, when He suffered He threatened not, that He was dumb, as a sheep before its shearers, is held up to us as an example. Temptation implies the possibility of sin. If from the constitution of His person it was impossible for Christ to sin, His temptation was unreal and without effect, and He cannot sympathize with His people.

~ Charles Hodge. *Systematic Theology, Abridged Edition.*
Edward N. Gross, ed. Grand Rapids: Baker Book House, 1992. p. 364-365.

The second development [in patristic theology] was the shift from affirming the fact that Christ did not sin to affirming that He could not sin. This was an extension of Augustinian ideas, and it shows how far the tradition had departed from the New Testament. Not only did this belief result in some theologians asserting that Christ did not take on a human nature identical to ours but only one which was analogous, but it also demanded that some account be given of how Christ's "impossible" temptations could be meritorious.

~ B. E. Foster. "Sinlessness of Christ."
Sinclair B. Ferguson, David F. Wright, J. I. Packer. Eds.
New Dictionary of Theology.
Downers Grove: InverVarsity Press, 1988. p. 643.

Did Jesus have the ability to sin? The problem hidden in that question is that if Jesus did have the ability to sin, does that mean He had original sin and participated in a fallen nature? If that were the case, He wouldn't even be qualified to save Himself, let alone us. If He did not have the ability to sin, was His temptation (so central to God's giving him the crown of glory for his obedience) just a charade – was He really not subjected to real temptation?

The New Testament tells us that Jesus was like us at every point save one: He was without sin. It tells us that Jesus became incarnate and took upon Himself sinful nature. It also tells us that He is the second Adam. Generally, classical Christology teaches that when Jesus was incarnate and became the new Adam, He came born with the same nature that Adam had before the Fall. Adam didn't have original sin when He was created. So Jesus did not have original sin. So we would

Theological Support for the Position that Jesus Could Have Sinned Had He Chosen to Do So, continued

ask the same question: Was Adam capable of sinning? Yes, he was. Christ, the second Adam, was also capable of sinning in the sense that He had all of the faculties and all of the equipment necessary to sin if that's what He chose to do.

Could Jesus have sinned if He had wanted to? Absolutely. Of course He didn't want to. So if you ask it a different way, could Jesus sin if He didn't want to? No, He couldn't sin if He didn't want to any more than God could sin because God doesn't want to sin. Wanting to sin is a prerequisite for sinning.

But then we have to push it one step further: Could Jesus have wanted to sin? Theologians are divided on this point. I would say yes, I think He could have. I think that's part of being made after the likeness of Adam. When we're in heaven and are totally glorified, then we will no longer have the power and ability to sin. That's what we look forward to; that's what Jesus earned for Himself and for us through His perfect obedience. Christ's perfect obedience was not a charade. He actually was victorious over every conceivable temptation that was thrown His way.

~ R. C. Sproul. URL: *www.fni.com/heritage/nov96/sproul.html*

Reprinted with permission at this web site from *Now, That's a Good Question!* **Published by Tyndale House Publishers.**

Appendix 40
The Tabernacle of Moses
Vern Poythress, *The Shadow of Christ in the Law of Moses*, p. 17.

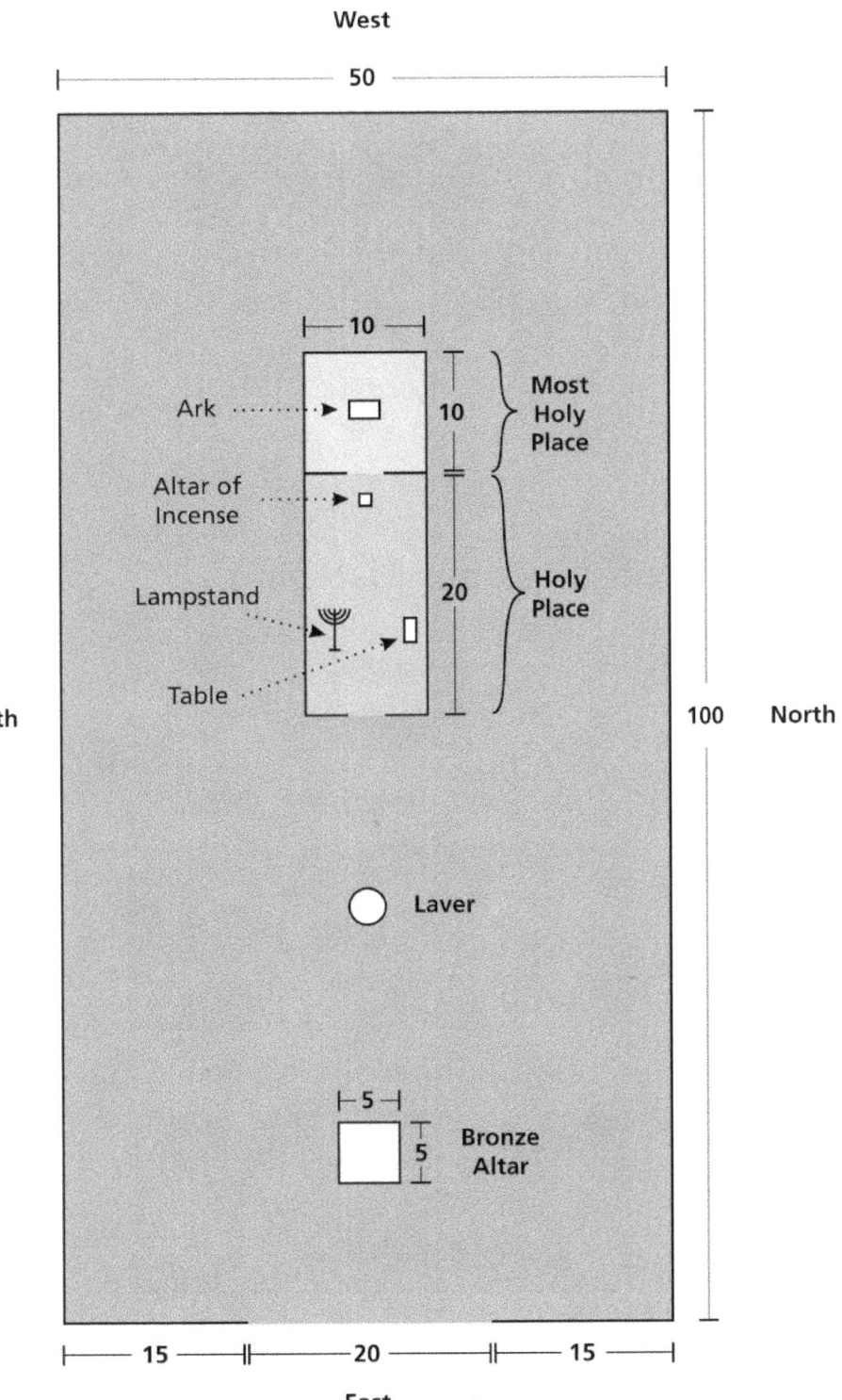

Appendix 41
Arrangement of the Twelve Tribes around the Tabernacle
Vern Poythress, *The Shadow of Christ in the Law of Moses.*

Tribes Encamped

```
                            Dan
  Manasseh                                          Issachar
           Asher                      Naphtali
  Ephraim           [ TABERNACLE ]                  Judah
           Simeon                     Gad
  Benjamin                                          Zebulon
                           Reuben
```

Tribes Marching

[ARK]

Zebulon Issachar Judah

[TABERNACLE MATERIAL
(Gershon, Merari)]

Gad Simeon Reuben

[TABERNACLE FURNITURE
(Kohath)]

Benjamin Manasseh Ephraim
Naphtali Asher Dan

Appendix 42
The Two Movements of Christ's Revelation: The Humiliation and Exaltation of the Son of God
Rev. Dr. Don L. Davis

He Came

From the throne of God above

Phil. 2.5-7a – Have this mind among yourselves, which is yours in Christ Jesus, [6] who, though he was in the form of God, did not count equality with God a thing to be grasped, [7] but made himself nothing, taking the form of a servant, being born in the likeness of men. And being found in human form,

Humiliation

He Died

Phil. 2.7-8 – but made himself nothing, taking the form of a servant, being born in the likeness of men. And being found in human form, [8] he humbled himself by becoming obedient to the point of death, even death on a cross.

"He descended into hell"
~ The Apostles' Creed

He Rose!

Phil. 2.9-11 – Therefore God has highly exalted him and bestowed on him the name that is above every name, [10] so that at the name of Jesus every knee should bow, in heaven and on earth and under the earth, [11] and every tongue confess that Jesus Christ is Lord, to the glory of God the Father.

- The *proof* of divinity
- The *power* of humility
- The *pattern* of spirituality
- The *purpose* of history
- The *prism* of veracity (truth)

Exaltation

He Will *Return!*

Mark 14.62 – And Jesus said, "I am, and you will see the Son of Man seated at the right hand of Power, and coming with the clouds of heaven."

To the right hand of the Father

Appendix 43
The Mystery of God: The Word Made Flesh in Jesus Christ
Rev. Dr. Don L. Davis

2 Cor. 4.6 – For God, who said, "Let light shine out of darkness," has shone in our hearts to give the light of the knowledge of the glory of God in the face of Jesus Christ.

Rom. 5.8 – but God shows his love for us in that while we were still sinners, Christ died for us.

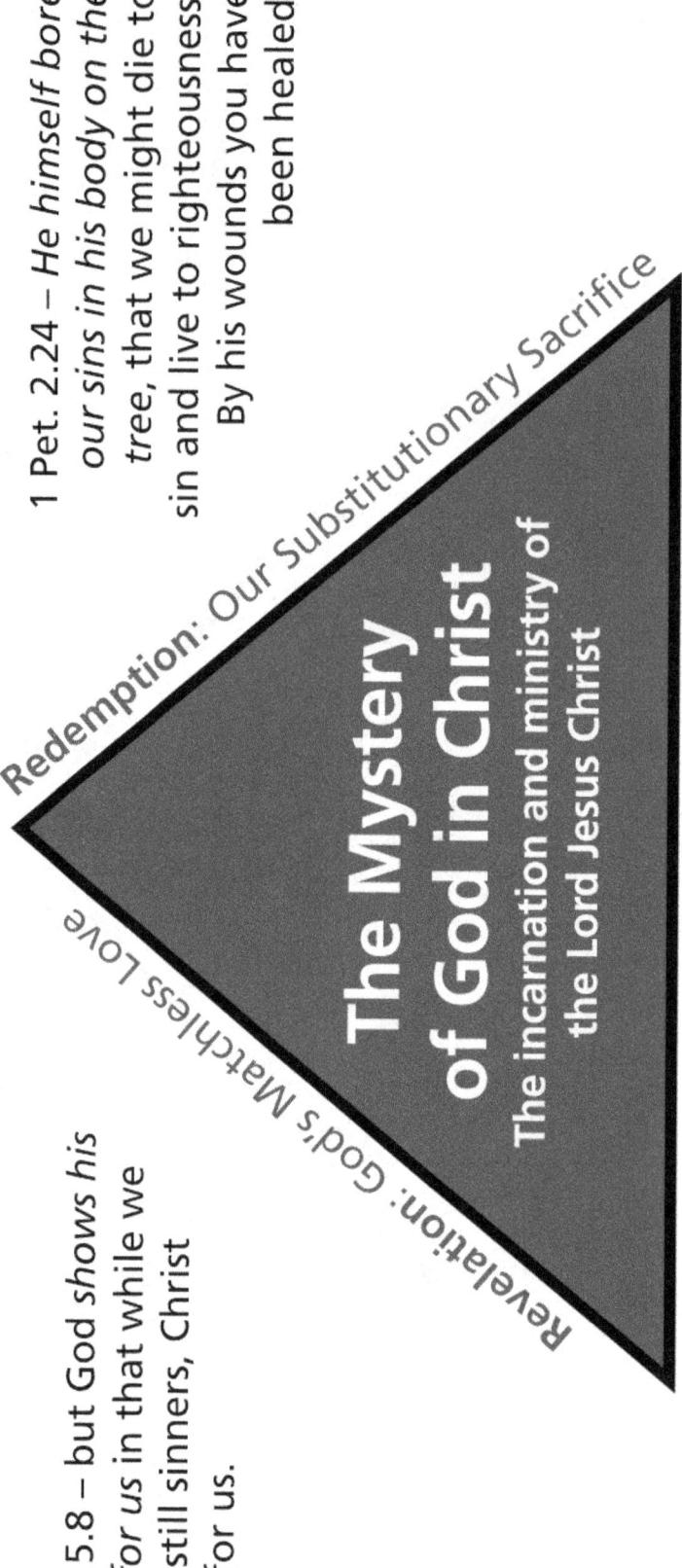

1 Pet. 2.24 – He himself bore our sins in his body on the tree, that we might die to sin and live to righteousness. By his wounds you have been healed.

1 John 3.8 – Whoever makes a practice of sinning is of the devil, for the devil has been sinning from the beginning. *The reason the Son of God appeared was to destroy the works of the devil.*

Appendix 44
The Risen Messiah Himself Is Our Life
Rev. Dr. Don L. Davis

> If then you have been raised with Christ,
>   seek the things that are above,
>   where Christ is, seated at the right hand of God.
> Set your minds on things that are above,
>   not on things that are on earth.
> For you have died, and your life is hidden with Christ in God.
>
> When Christ who is your life appears,
>   then you also will appear with him in glory.
>
> ~ Colossians 3.1-4

Let us keep in mind that instead of giving us one object after another, God gives His Son to us. Because of this, we can always lift up our hearts and look to the Lord, saying, "Lord, You are my way; Lord, You are my truth; Lord, You are my life. It is you, Lord, who is related to me, not your things." May we ask God to give us grace that we may see Christ in all spiritual things. Day by day we are convinced that aside from Christ there is no way, nor truth, nor life. How easily we make things as way, truth, and life. Or, we call hot atmosphere as life, we label clear thought as life. We consider strong emotion or outward conduct as life. In reality, though, these are not life. We ought to realize that only the Lord is life Christ is our life. And it is the Lord who lives out this life in us. Let us ask Him to deliver us from the many external and fragmentary affairs that we may touch only Him. May we see the Lord in all things – way, truth, and life are all found in knowing Him. May we really meet the Son of God and let Him live in us. Amen.

~ Watchman Nee. *Christ, the Sum of All Spiritual Things*. New York: Christian Fellowship Publishers, 1973. p. 20.

Appendix 45
Major Heresies Concerning the Lord Jesus Christ
Rev. Dr. Don L. Davis

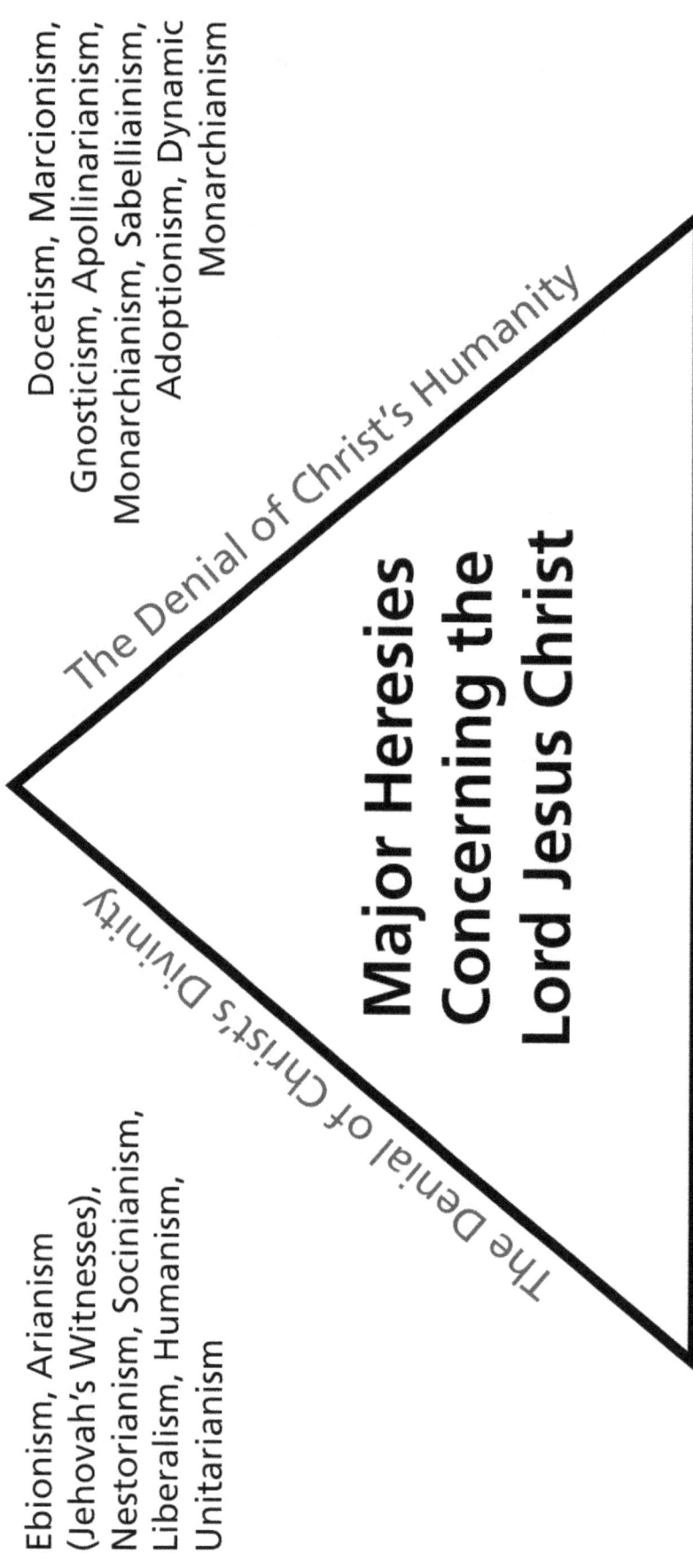

Major Heresies Concerning the Lord Jesus Christ

The Denial of Christ's Humanity: Docetism, Marcionism, Gnosticism, Apollinarianism, Monarchianism, Sabellianism, Adoptionism, Dynamic Monarchianism

The Denial of Christ's Divinity: Ebionism, Arianism (Jehovah's Witnesses), Nestorianism, Socinianism, Liberalism, Humanism, Unitarianism

The Denial of Christ's Two Natures: Monophystism, Eutychianism, Monthelitiesm

Bibliography
The Epistle to the Hebrews: Part I

Allsman, Don. *Jesus Cropped from the Picture: Why Christians Get Bored and How to Restore them to Vibrant Faith.* Wichita, KS: The Urban Ministry Institute Press, 2009.

Aulen, Gustaf. *Christus Victor.* Trans. A. G. Hebert. New York: Collier Books, 1969.

Baron, David. *Rays of Messiah's Glory: Christ in the Old Testament.* Eugene, OR: Wipf and Stock Publishers, 2001.

Barrett, Michael. *Beginning at Moses: A Guide to Finding Christ in the Old Testament.* Greenville, SC: Ambassador-Emerald International, 1999.

Baxter, J. Sidlow. *The Master Theme of the Bible.* 2nd ed. Grand Rapids: Kregel Publications, 1997.

Beasley-Murray, G. R. *Jesus and the Kingdom of God.* Grand Rapids: Eerdmans, 1986.

Bonhoeffer, Dietrich. *Christ, the Center.* Trans. Edwin H. Robertson. San Francisco: Harper and Row Publishers, 1978.

Borland, James A. *Christ in the Old Testament: Old Testament Appearances of Christ in Human Form.* Rev. and expanded ed. Ross-shire: Mentor, 1999.

Brown, Raymond. *Jesus, God and Man: Modern Biblical Reflections.* New York, Paulist Press, 1980.

———. *The Birth of the Messiah.* New York: Doubleday, 1979.

———. *The Death of the Messiah.* New York: Doubleday, 1994.

Brueggemann, Walter. *The Prophetic Imagination.* (Rev. and updated ed.) Minneapolis, MN: Augsburg Fortress Publishers, 2001.

———. *Hopeful Imagination: Prophetic Voices in Exile.* Minneapolis, MN: Augsburg Fortress Publishers, 1986.

Clowney, Edmund P. *Preaching Christ in All Scripture*. Wheaton, IL:Crossway Books, 2003.

———. *The Unfolding Mystery: Discovering Christ in the Old Testament*. Phillipsburg, NJ: P & R Publishing, 1991.

Conner, Kevin J. *Interpreting the Symbols and Types*. Rev. ed. Portland, OR: City Christian Publishing; 1999.

Davis, Don L. *God the Son*. Module 10: The Capstone Curriculum. Wichita, KS: The Urban Ministry Institute Press, 2005.

———.Davis, Don L. *Sacred Roots: A Primer on Retrieving the Great Tradition*. Wichita, KS: The Urban Ministry Institute Press, 2010.

———. *The New Testament Witness to Christ and His Kingdom*. Module 13: The Capstone Curriculum. Wichita, KS: The Urban Ministry Institute Press, 2005.

———. *The Old Testament Witness to Christ and His Kingdom*. Module 9: The Capstone Curriculum. Wichita, KS: The Urban Ministry Institute Press, 2005.

Demarest, Bruce A. *Jesus Christ: The God-Man*. Eugene: Wipf and Stock Publishers, 2004.

DeYoung, James, and Sarah Hurty. *Beyond the Obvious: Discovering the Deeper Meaning of Scripture*. Gresham, OR: Vision House Publishing, 1995.

Dodd, C. H. *The Founder of Christianity*. New York: Macmillan, 1970.

Drew, Charles D. *The Ancient Love Song: Finding Christ in the Old Testament*. Phillipsburg, NJ: P & R Publishing, 2000.

Dunnett, Walter M. *Exploring the New Testament*. Wheaton: Evangelical Training Association, 2001.

Fairbairn, Patrick. *The Typology of Scripture*. 2 vols. Reprint. Grand Rapids: Baker Books, 1975.

Fee, Gordon D. and Douglas Stuart. *How to Read the Bible for All Its Worth*. Grand Rapids: Zondervan Publishing, 2003.

Fredriksen, Paula. *From Jesus to Christ: The Origin of the New Testament Images of Jesus*. New York: Oxford University Press, 1988.

Geisler, Norman L. *A Popular Survey of the Old Testament*. Grand Rapids: Baker Book House, 2003.

———. *To Understand the Bible Look for Jesus*. Eugene: Wipf and Stock Publishers, 2002.

Greidanus, Sidney. *Preaching Christ from the Old Testament: A Contemporary Hermeneutical Method*. Grand Rapids: Wm. B. Eerdmans Publishing Company, 1999.

Habershon, Ada R. *Study of the Types*. Grand Rapids: Kregel Publishing, 1997.

Hoehner, Harold W. *Chronological Aspects of the Life of Christ*. Grand Rapids: Zondervan, 1977.

Hunter, Archibald M. *The Work and Words of Jesus*. Rev. ed. Philadelphia: The Westminster Press, 1973.

Kaiser, Walter C., Jr. *The Messiah in the Old Testament*. Grand Rapids: Zondervan, 1995.

———. *Preaching and Teaching from the Old Testament*. Grand Rapids: Baker Academic Books, 2003.

Kiehl, Erich H. *The Passion of Our Lord*. Grand Rapids: Baker Book House, 1990.

Ladd, George Eldon. *I believe in the Resurrection of Jesus*. Grand Rapids: Eerdmans, 1975.

———. *Jesus and the Kingdom*. New York: Harper, 1964.

———. *The Last Things*. Grand Rapids: Eerdmans, 1978.

———. *The Presence of the Future*. Rev. Ed. Grand Rapids: Eerdmans, 1974.

Lohse, Eduard. *History of the Suffering and Death of Jesus Christ*. Philadelphia: Fortrestt Press, 1967.

Longman, Tremper, III. *Immanuel in Our Place: Seeing Christ in Israel's Worship*. Phillipsburg, NJ: P & R Publishing, 2001.

Meier, John P. *A Marginal Jew: Rethinking the Historical Jesus*. New York: Doubleday, 1991.

Poythress, Vern S. *The Shadow of Christ in the Law of Moses*. Phillipsburg, NJ: P & R Publishing, 1991.

Roberts, Vaughan. *God's Big Picture: Tracing the Storyline of the Bible*. Downers Grove, Ill.: InterVarsity Books, 2002.

Robertson, O. Palmer. *The Christ of the Prophets*. Phillipsburg, NJ: P & R Publishing, 2004.

———. *Christ of the Covenants*. Phillipsburg, NJ: P & R Publishing, 1981.

Ryken, Leland. *How to Read the Bible as Literature and Get More Out of It*. Grand Rapids: Zondervan Publishing, 1984.

Spurgeon, Charles H. *Christ in the Old Testament: Sermons on the Foreshadowings of Our Lord in Old Testament History, Ceremony, and Prophecy*. (Pulpit Legend Collection). Chattanooga, TN: AMG Publishers, 2001.

Stott, John R. W. *Life in Christ*. 2nd ed. Grand Rapids: Baker Books, 1996.

———. *The Cross of Christ*. Downers Grove: InterVarsity Press, 1986.

———. *The Incomparable Christ*. Downers Grove: InterVarsity Press, 2001.

Wald, Oletta. *The New Joy of Discovery in Bible Study*. Rev. ed. Minneapolis: Augsburg Fortress, 2002.

Wilson, Walter L. *A Dictionary of Bible Types*. Peabody, MS: Hendrickson Publishers, 1999.

Wright, Christopher J. H. *Knowing Jesus through the Old Testament*. Downers Grove: InterVarsity Press, 1992.

About Us

Many urban churches and ministries suffer with discouragement because there is little lasting fruit. Often there is no plan for leadership development. The biggest obstacle to successfully planting churches is training indigenous leaders to be pastors, to be able to rightly divide the Word of Truth without losing their cultural distinctive. For decades the Church in America has told the urban poor, "If you want a theological education, you have to change cultures and know someone who is rich." We have basically said, "Do not bother to apply to get Bible training." Consequently, biblically sound, evangelical urban leadership is uncommon.

The Urban Ministry Institute (TUMI) overcomes four barriers that urban leaders face in their efforts to receive theological education:

1. *Cost*: Many urban pastors could never afford to attend a traditional seminary.

2. *Academic requirements*: Many of God's chosen leaders in the inner city have little more than a high school education and would not be admitted to most seminaries.

3. *Proximity*: Most urban leaders have a full-time ministry, a family, and a full-time job, so uprooting their family and abandoning their ministry to go away to Bible college is out of the question.

4. *Cultural relevance*: Most of what is taught in traditional seminaries does not equip an urban pastor to lead a flock in the inner city, so even if he/she could afford to go to Bible school, what is taught there is not relevant to daily life.

In 1995 we launched TUMI in Wichita, Kansas, and have equipped hundreds of pastors since then. In 2000 we began establishing satellite training centers in other inner cities across the country and around the world. We have satellites in partnership with denominations, ministries, and schools, hosted in such places as churches, missions, prisons, and seminaries, and located all over the United States with international partners in places such as Canada, Puerto Rico, Ghana, Guatemala, Mexico, Pakistan, and Liberia. Check our website www.tumi.org for all of our satellite locations.

We offer a variety of training materials and resources (visit *www.tumi.org*). Take advantage of our rich experience in church planting, urban ministry, and evangelism by ordering resources for your church or personal ministry. These can be used in your church, Sunday school class, small group or personal study.

- Sermons
- Prayer devotionals (series) and resources to lead groups in prayer concerts
- The Capstone Curriculum: courses on DVD with Student Workbooks and Mentor Guides
- Artwork for the urban church
- Books and workbooks with built-in study questions

Helping Churches to Rediscover Vital Spirituality!

We believe that in order to renew our personal and corporate walks in the contemporary church we must simply return and rediscover our Sacred Roots, i.e., the core beliefs, practices, and commitments of the Christian faith. These roots are neither sectarian nor provincial, but are rather cherished and recognized by all believers everywhere, at all times, and by everyone. Paul exhorted the Thessalonians, "So then, brothers, stand firm and hold to the traditions that you were taught by us, either by our spoken word or by our letter" (2 Thess. 2.15). Our Sacred Roots necessarily suggest that all who believe (wherever and whenever they have lived) affirm their common rootedness in the saving work of God, the same Lord who created, covenanted with Israel, was incarnate in Christ, and is being witnessed to by his people, the Church.

Jesus Cropped from the Picture
Why Christians Get Bored and How to Restore Them to Vibrant Faith
by Rev. Don Allsman

Why are many churches shrinking? Why are so many Christians bored? Could it be that the well-meaning attempt to simplify the gospel message for contemporary culture has produced churches full of discouraged people secretly longing for something more? *Jesus Cropped from the Picture* describes this phenomenon and proposes a return to our sacred roots as a guard against spiritual lethargy and a way to enhance spiritual vibrancy.

Sacred Roots
A Primer on Retrieving the Great Tradition
by Dr. Don L. Davis

The Christian Faith is anchored on the person and work of Jesus of Nazareth, the Christ, whose incarnation, crucifixion, and resurrection forever changed the world. Between the years 100 and 500 C.E. those who believed in him grew from a small persecuted minority to a strong aggressive movement reaching far beyond the bounds of the Roman empire. The roots this era produced gave us our canon (the Scriptures), our worship, and our conviction (the major creeds of the Church, and the central tenets of the Faith, especially regarding the doctrine of the Trinity and Christ). This book suggests how we can renew our contemporary faith again, by rediscovering these roots, our Sacred Roots, by retrieving the Great Tradition of the Church that launched the Christian revolution.

Participating in Urban Church Planting Movements

If you are interested in more of Dr. Davis's ideas on how to facilitate or participate in urban church planting movements and how you can help sustain them through retrieving the Great Tradition, be sure to get your own copies of the following three *Foundations for Ministry Series* courses. These three courses are central to discussing what we understand the focus of urban mission to be, both in terms of the aim of it (i.e., to multiply churches rapidly among the urban poor), and the substance of it (i.e., retrieving and expressing The Great Tradition with churches that contextualize it).

Winning the World: Facilitating Urban Church Planting Movements
At a time when our definitions of the Church have become more and more individualized, this study analyzes church plant and growth theories as they relate to the more communal Nicene-based marks of church life. Using these marks as the basis for a more biblical view of the Church, this study discusses and investigates the connection between church planting, world evangelization, church growth, leadership development, and urban mission. It clearly identifies the underlying principles which have contributed to the explosive multiplication of churches in places like India, Latin America, and China, and proposes the possibility of similar movements of revival, renewal, and reproduction among the poor in American cities. This course lays the foundation for the necessary principles underlying key elements of a Church Planting Movement and what it would take to facilitate and participate in one [workbook and MP3 audio – visit *www.tumi.org/foundations*].

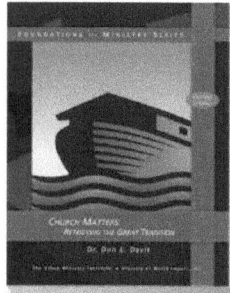

Church Matters: Retrieving the Great Tradition

At a time of turbulence and dramatic change in society and uneasiness and compromise in the Church, it is critical for believers to retain a sense of the history of the body of Christ. What is needed today is a sense of perspective, i.e., coming to view and understand current events through the lens of God's working through the Church through the ages. Armed with a sense of history, we will be both encouraged and challenged that our current situation is neither unique nor unresolvable. Through the great movements of the Church, the Holy Spirit has shown that even in the face of schism, compromise, difficulty, and persecution, the people of God can learn, grow, and fulfill God's plan for them. This course shows that you can rediscover the power of the living biblical tradition of the Church, anchored in the person and work of Jesus Christ, and how essential it is to ground our Church Planting on something larger than us. Throughout its history, the Church has proven that God's unique plan can unfold even in the face of schism and persecution. Such wisdom is critical to renew and revive the urban church today [workbook and MP3 audio – visit *www.tumi.org/foundations*].

Marking Time: Forming Spirituality through the Christian Year

In this course, we explore the origins and meaning of the Christian Year and how it represents the profound yet simple remembrance and re-enactment of the life of Christ in real time during the calendar year. Beginning with an overview of the Bible's teaching in connection to time and history, this course explores the dominant view of the atonement, Christus Victor, which reigned in the ancient Church for a thousand years. We look at how this dynamic vision of Jesus' victory over sin and death was captured in the worship of the Church in the Church Year. This course, then, lays out the argument and rationale for embracing the Church Year as a structure that enables us to enhance spiritual formation in the urban church setting [workbook and MP3 audio – visit *www.tumi.org/foundations*].

www.ingramcontent.com/pod-product-compliance
Lightning Source LLC
Chambersburg PA
CBHW080544090426
42734CB00016B/3192